FLOATING CLOUDS
CHINESE-ENGLISH RHYMED VERSE

浮云集
汉英双语诗韵

作者与翻译: 余新
Author & Translator: Yu Xin

CHICAGO ACADEMIC PRESS

FLOATING CLOUDS: CHINESE-ENGLISH RHYMED VERSE
Author & Translator: Yu Xin
Planner: Yu Qiang
Language: Chinese and English
Publisher: Chicago Academic Press, Jan 16, 2025
ISBN 978-1-965890-12-7

浮云集：汉英双语诗韵

作者与翻译: 余新

策划：余强

语　言: 中文、英文

出版社: 芝加哥学术出版社　2025 年 1 月 16 日

书　号 978-1-965890-12-7

Library of Congress Control Number: 2025930287

Publishing　Chicago Academic Press
　　　　　　Chicago Illinois
E-mail　　contact@chicagoacademicpress.com
Website　http://chicagoacademicpress.com/

Book Size　6X9 inches
First Edition January 16, 2025

作者与翻译: 余新
Author & Translator: Yu Xin

作者与译者简介

　　余新，笔名余心JANE，《中国红馆》执行总编，《中西诗鉴》主编，唐山诗词学会副会长。2019年获得中华诗词学会女工委年度佳诗之一，曾获美国诗殿堂评：Best Chinese Writer of Classical Poems，曾于世界诗歌联合总会获嘉奖。曾翻译于美国出版《汉译莎士比亚十四行诗》。

About the Author & Translator

　　Yu Xin, pen name Yu Xin JANE, is the executive chief editor of China Red Academy, chief editor of Chinese and Western Poetry Appreciation, the vice president of Tangshan Poetry Society. In 2019, her poem was chosen as one of the Best Poems of the Year by the Women's Working Committee of the Chinese Poetry Society, and she was chosen as the Best Chinese Writer of Classical Poems by the American Poetry Hall, and also awarded by the World Poetry Federation. She translated and published *Chinese Translation of William Shakespeare's Sonnets* in America.

自　序

　　诗者，心灵之鸣也，乃情感之精琢、深掘，更是对美之不懈求索。于岁月长河中，吾将诸多曾触动心灵、沉淀于心之点滴，视作滋养自身之甘腴，汇集成此双语诗集《浮云集:英汉双语诗韵》。

　　此部诗集内容，共分三章。首章乃吾倾心之作双语诗词，其间以亲情篇为重。亲情，乃吾生命之主轴，若生命中最和煦之港湾。亲人之逝，予吾无尽伤痛，恰似魔幻之巨网，令吾屡屡深陷，难以挣脱。正所谓"黯然销魂者，唯别而已矣"，唯文字，自笔端流出，方可舒缓压力，自救于困境，创作此双语诗词时，吾力臻展现诗词之节奏美韵。而综合篇，则为对生活、自然与人生之种种感怀，以诗之言语，铭记那些扣动心弦之瞬间。

　　次章，乃收录些近年吾所译近体诗词。唐诗宋词，是中华文化之璀璨明珠，蕴含无穷智慧和情愫。吾竭力在音节及韵脚上追求，翻译之际，力求以较好效果呈现作者本意，以便让更多人可领略中国近体诗词之魅力。

　　末章为部分欧美经典英诗之汉译。欧美诗歌，独具风格与表达方式，在翻译之际，吾努力跨越语言障碍，期望能让读者于汉语语境中感受别样诗意，恰似《诗经》云"他山之石，可以攻玉"。

　　诗乃世间最美之语言艺术，可穿越时空，触动人心深处之柔软。吾诚愿该诗集能架起一座桥梁，连接起不同语言和文化背景之读者，共同体会诗词之美好情愫，在文字广袤海洋中绽放光芒。由于本人水平有限，多有不足，敬请方家指正，鸣谢。

Preface

Poetry is the voice from the soul. It is the elaborate carving and deep exploration of emotions, and the ceaseless pursuit of beauty. Over the long years, I regarded many bits and pieces that once touched my soul and settled in my heart as the sweet nourishment for myself, and compiled them into this bilingual poetry collection, "Floating Clouds: Chinese-English Rhymed Verse".

The content of this poetry collection is divided into three chapters. The first chapter consists of the bilingual poems I created with devotion, among which the part about family affection is the most significant. Family affection is the core of my life, like the warmest harbour in life. The deaths of my loved ones have brought me endless grief, just like a magical and huge net, making me trapped time and again and unable to break free. Just as it is said, "The most heart-rending thing is parting." Only by having words flowing from my pen can I relieve the pressure and extricate myself from the predicament. When composing these bilingual poems, I strived to present the rhythm and wonderful charm of poetry. The comprehensive   part contains various sentiments about life, nature and human experiences, using the language of poetry to remember those moments that touch my heart.

The second chapter includes the recent translations of classical regulated verse and poetry I have made in recent years. Tang Poetry and Song Ci are the shining pearls in Chinese culture, containing boundless wisdom and emotions.
I did my best to pursue the syllables and rhymes. When translating, I strived to present the author's meaning with a better effect, so that more people can appreciate the charm of
Chinese classical regulated verse and poetry.

The third chapter is the Chinese translations of some classic English poems from Europe and America. European and American poems have unique styles and expressions. When translating them, I endeavored to overcome the language barrier, hoping to enable readers to experience different poetic sentiments in the Chinese language context, just like what is said in "The Book of Songs": "Stones from other mountains can be used to polish jade."

Poetry is the most beautiful language art in the world. It can traverse time and space and touch the softness deep in people's hearts. I sincerely hope that this poetry collection can build a bridge, connecting readers with different languages and cultural backgrounds, allowing them to jointly experience the beautiful emotions in poetry and shine in the vast ocean of words. Due to my limited ability, there are many deficiencies. I sincerely ask for corrections from experts. Thank you.

目　录
Contents

三、古诗词英译篇
Part III. English Translations of Classical Chinese Poetry ⋯⋯⋯⋯⋯⋯⋯⋯⋯⋯⋯⋯⋯⋯⋯⋯⋯⋯ **183**

四、英诗汉译篇
Part IV. Chinese Translation of English Poetry······ 291

（一）
亲情篇

Part I
Family Affection

原创诗词
Author's Original Poetry

1

长相思
老家

紫燕飞，
紫燕飞。
弱小年年入夏归，
一生老屋陪。

昨日追，
昨日追。
涉远他乡风月随，
人衰夜色垂。

1

To the Tune of
Chang Xiang Si
My Hometown

The purple swallows fly,
The purple swallows fly.
Weak and tiny, they return in summer each year;
All their lives they are with the old house here.

Th' pursuit of yesterday,
Th' pursuit of yesterday.
Far away in a foreign land, with moon and wind,
As one ages, the nightfall falls I find.

2

西江月
题女儿阔轩深圳创业

五彩青春明丽，
千金妙景幽妍。
春风抚处勇无前，
细抹繁华入卷。

笔拓胸怀蓝宇，
墨成才调红颜。
鹏城雄壮奉佳篇，
弘毅今朝看遍。

2

To the Tune of
Xi Jiang Yue
On My Daughter Kuo Xuan's Entrepreneurship
in Shenzhen

Your colorful youth is shining and gorgeous;
Your precious vision is charming and serene.
Wherever the spring breeze blows, you march with brave
sheen,
Carefully portray prosperous views in th' scene.

Your pen extends the vast blue sky in your mind,
And shows the talents and grace with ink so fair.
You showcase fine works in grand Shenzhen everywhere;
Your resolute spirit is always so rare.

3

西江月
祝贺女儿阔轩入编国家小学美术教材

执笔青山如踏，
临风皓月堪邀。
田园广阔用心描，
拔地神州怀抱。

为筑百年人气，
当培一代春苗。
暗香浸透育花桃，
慧识育根英少。

3

To the Tune of
Xi Jiang Yue
Congratulating My Daughter Kuo Xuan on Her Inclusion in the Chinese Primary School Art Textbook

Holding the brush, you're like treading on green
mountains;
Facing the wind, you could invite moon clear and bright.
The vast countryside needs to be drawn with care all right;
You embrace the land of China with pride outright.

To build the vitality for a hundred years,
We should nurture the sprouts of a generation.
As faint scents soak through flowers and peaches'
gestation;
You nourish the young talents with inspiration.

4

西江月
题女儿阔轩深圳科技馆设计竣工

展翅大鹏深圳，
乘风唱响乾坤。
合盘经济领衔身，
展馆必须先进。

数字文明充分，
多重科技皆新。
网红打卡汇精神，
小女获称奇隽。

4

To the Tune of
Xi Jiang Yue
On the Completion of My Daughter Kuo Xuan's Design for Shenzhen Science and Technology Museum

Shenzhen is like a roc spreading its wings;
Riding the wind, throughout the world it sings.
At the forefront of the integrated economy ,
The design of th' museum must be trendy.

Digital culture is quite fully shown;
Many brand-new technologies are known.
It serves as an internet- famous check-in spot with soul;
My daughter is hailed as a great girl throughout th' whole.

5

江城子
清明祭扫父母

疫情三载剩清风。
草蓬蓬，念无停。
青冥尤见，丽日映愁踪。
新土润坟安可寄？
四子女，泪如倾。

5

To the Tune of
Jiang Cheng Zi
Paying Respect to My Parents at Their Tomb on the Qingming Festival

Three years of the plague have passed,the breeze lingers
still;
The grass there is lush, my longing never goes nil.
In the blue sky, the bright sun casts the traces of grief still.
How can new soil covering the tomb bear our grief?
The four children, tears streaming down like rain at will.

6

江城子
腊八节怀父

为寻来处苦无舟。
鸟儿啾，锁烟愁。
家门不见，慈父哪方求。
夜幕沧桑淹厚土，
神暗度，爱长留。

6

To the Tune of
Jiang Cheng Zi
In Memory of My Father on the Laba Festival

In search of my origin, yet no boat can lead the way,
Birds chirp and play, while sorrow veils my heart like
smoke grey.
My home door isn't in sight,where can I find my father
today?
The night's veil of vicissitudes covers the thick earth,
His love remains forever, though his soul passed away.

7

促拍采桑子
念余江长兄

前夜雨相催。
打窗棂、疑长兄回。
儿时不解，
离离散散，
堪比天垂。

历变人间增一恨，
噬娘心、寒气重围。
朝朝暮暮，
欢声遁杳，
卅载星亏。

7

To the Tune of
Cu Pai Cai Sang Zi
In Memory of my Eldest Brother Yu Jiang

The rain came down on the previous night.
Beating windows, I guessed my brother came alright.
As a child, I didn't understand,
The separation and dispersion,
Rivaling the collapse of th' skylight.

The changes in the human world have added a grudge,
Piercing my mother's heart amid th' chilly siege blight.
Day after day and night after night,
The voices of joy have vanished,
For forty years, the stars have dimmed light.

8

促拍采桑子
青龙湖畔忆仲兄

青叶对长空。
柳拂心、淹没凄清。
飘然已逝，
莲台泪眼，遥望云横。

黯路昏天遗憾意，
嫂相寻、兄影千重。
痴红泣血，
殷殷寂色，
倒染无穷。

8

To the Tune of
Cu Pai Cai Sang Zi
In Memory of My Second Elder Brother by
Qinglong Lake

The green leaves face the boundless sky.
Willows soothe th' heart and drown my sorrows with a
sigh.
You passed away so fleetingly;
With tearful eyes by th' lotus throne,
I watch afar as the clouds fly.

Regretting,in the gloomy road and dusky sky,
My sister-in-law seeks your figure frequently.
The spoony blooms shed blood-like tears;
The thick and solitary tint,
stains the human world endlessly.

9

七绝
念双亲
（新韵）

连日恍惚思虑缠，
申时小睡梦椿萱。
孤愁良父来相助，
仰望空中是彩天。

注：申时，是中国传统十二时辰之一。

9

A Seven-Character Quatrain
Missing My Late Parents
(New Rhyme)

For some days I have been in a trance of deep woe,
Dreaming of my late parents during the Shen time.
My father helped me when I felt lonely sorrow;
When looking up, I find it's the glorious prime.

Note: The Shen time is one of the twelve traditional
Chinese two-hour periods.

10

七绝
寄双亲
（新韵）

难忘绵长父母恩，
一腔心血注儿身。
今朝春色又添锦，
暗落惊鸿滋味沉。

10

A Seven-Character Quatrain
Dedicated to My Late Parents
(New Rhyme)

I will never forget my parents' boundless grace;
Their hearts' blood was devoted to my growing place.
Today, the spring scenery gains more charm and hue;
Like startled wild geese passing, I am in a mood blue.

11

游四门
中元节

中元两界扼花机，
　地府放魂归。
生灵能懂相思意，
　哭诉慰亲知。
　　悲，
遥念越空兮！

11

To the Tune of
You Si Men
On the Mid-July Ghost Festival

At Zhongyuan, two realms, mortals and Hades, hold back
flowers' bloom;
The netherworld releases souls from hell's gloom.
The living can understand the essence of the yearning,
To console their dear ones with weeping an' mourning.
So sorrowful!
Through the endless space is that distant longing.

12

江城子
2024 年 10 月 1 日祭亲

心潮卷过苦拥胸。
日无明，半宵风。
亲人何在？今日赴坟茔。
天冷寒衣冥纸寄，
呼父母，望良兄。

12

To the Tune of
Jiang Cheng Zi
Memorial for My Relatives on October 1st, 2024
in the Lunar Calendar

My heart surges, and bitterness enfolds my chest.
The sun is veiled in haze, and for half the night winds did
wrest.
Where have my loved ones gone? I'm heading for the
graves today.
It's cold, I send them clothes and Joss paper on th' way;
I cry for my parents an' yearn for my elder bro, I pray.

13

减字木兰花
故居丁香

房前亭立，
一片幽香时破寂。
挤入窗棂，
掀起芬芳满户盈。

光阴远去，
常念丁香难又聚。
梦中回乡，
余味犹如还绕梁。

13

To the Tune of
Jian Zi Mu Lan Hua
The Lilacs of My Old Home

Before the house they stood straight,
Now and then, a waft of scent broke the silent state.
Squeezing through the pane so fair,
It raised a burst of aroma and filled the air.

All the time has passed away;
I often miss the lilacs, but hardly meet today.
I returned home in my dreams;
The remaining scent seems to linger round th' roof beams.

14

七律
腊八节忆父
（新韵）

西风今日若冰寒，
面对萧竹把酒酣。
一阙荒烟铭志远，
无边落日记时艰。
云飘纱荡惊天帝，
夜坠更思忆旧颜。
父语连心薄梦寄，
平安顺遂泪潸然。

14

A Seven-Character Octave
Recalling My Father on Laba Festival
(New Rhyme)

The west wind is as cold as ice today;
Facing the bleak bamboos, very drunk I'm.
With th' smoke in th' wild, I've made my will strong aye;
The setting sun afar marks th' past hard time.
The God is amazed at the voile-like cloud;
When night fell, I missed my dad's face of yore.
In my light dream my dad's words made me proud,
Shedding tears I wish he were safe still more.

15

江城子
纪念母亲逝世 36 周年

母亲一逝宿青川。
渺尘烟，复难还。
三十六载，缺月永魂牵。
茕立人间风起日，
神倍苦，语凝咽。

15

To the Tune of
Jiang Cheng Zi
In Memory of the 36th Anniversary of My
Mother's Passing

My mom rests in the green plain after passing away.
Admist the dust and smoke, she's never back anyway.
For thirty-six years, the crescent moon haunts my soul all
the way.
When I stand alone in this world on a windy day,
My mind is in deep pain and my words choke when I say.

16

七绝
致余强兄

男儿毅力抵洪流，
风浪劈波排尽愁。
滋味蝉联知百苦，
得来甘露脱牢囚。

16

A Seven-Character Quatrain
Ode to My Elder Brother Yu Qiang

A man's will power can stand up against the flood;
Like the wind breaking waves, dispel worries you would.
Through successive experiences you know much pain;
Getting rid of the prison, the sweet dews you gain.

17

七绝
致余强兄

左首青山右首瓯，
男儿意志抵洪流。
今朝无惧祛疾苦，
日日安康奇迹求。

17

A Seven-Character Quatrain
To My Elder Brother Yu Qiang

On your left is green hill and right the cup;
A man's will can withstand the mighty flood.
Now you're so brave to make th' illness heal up;
Be safe each day as a marvel you would.

18

七绝
题画家阔轩生日

初春嫩蕊绽金辉，
陪伴轩轩日子肥。
转眼经年儿长大，
翩然笔下凤凰飞。

18

A Seven-Character Quatrain
A Poem for the Birthday of the Painter Kuo Xuan

In early spring the young buds bloom in gold sunlight,
Accompanying Xuan Xuan who enjoys a life fine.
In a matter of years my child's grown up alright;
A phoenix in flight is drawn by the brush of thine.

19

七绝
小年念儿
（新韵）

小年终日想儿归，
公务缠身未可回。
蒸好一锅香米饭，
相思佐味看烟炊。

19

A Seven-Character Quatrain
Missing My Daughter on Minor New Year
(New Rhyme)

I miss my daughter all day on Minor New Year;
On official duty she can't return here.
I've steamed a pot of tasty rice with love and care;
With yearning as taste I watch steam rise in the air.

20

七绝
母亲节惠题小女

愿儿如月映光辉，
持伴欢歌载玉杯。
修道天公疼爱女，
房前屋后送玫瑰。

20

A Seven-Character Quatrain
The Poem for My Daughter on Mother's Day

May my daughter shine as bright as the moon;
To sing with friends, holding jade cups, she's boon .
The providential God loves my dear girl,
And sends roses around her house so soon.

21

七绝
题二姐余英生日

生辰吉日祝祥安，
福气冲天花满园。
多少琼思多少事，
一身康健不忧烦。

21

A Seven-Character Quatrain
A Poem for the Birthday of My Second Elder Sister Yu Ying

On th' auspicious birthday, I wish you luck and peace;
The garden's full of flowers as blessings abound.
How many lovely thoughts and matters have you found?
I only hope you are healthy and all cares cease.

22

七绝
大舅父

舅父治家百事昌，
儿孙孝道品贤良。
心胸宽广无难事，
话出谦辞如律章。

22

A Seven-Character Quatrain
My Eldest Maternal Uncle

My uncle governs the family very well;
His offsprings are filial and morally fine.
Free from troubles his heart is broad; he doesn't pine;
As orderly as rules his humble words sound swell.

23

七绝
赞二姑妈

雨露花沾归绣楼，
芳菲一院近相酬。
儒风卫道含家国，
仁爱慈心带义柔。

23

A Seven-Character Quatrain
Ode to My Second Aunt

When blooms were dewy you're back to th' boudoir of
thine;
You draw close to the flowers in the yard so fine.
You bear a Confucian heart for our home and state;
You're a person so kind, righteous, gentle and great.

（二）
综合篇

Part II
Comprehensive Collection

原创诗词

Author's Original Poetry

24

七律
人生偶感

辗转春秋恰似鸥，
清风飘荡几争流。
红尘落落扛身骨，
雾野飞飞唱世愁。
辍罢兰心知卤味，
敲轻黄叶动霜眸。
晴姿每有寒姿近，
渤海兴帆去放舟。

24

A Seven-Character Octave
Occasional Feelings in My Life

I spend spring an' fall like a sea gull in squall;
The cool breeze flutters and struggles to flow.
I hold up my bones when things rise and fall;
In th' mist around fields I sing worldly woe.
My heart's not like orchids to taste th' bitter;
I hit the brown leaves but move eyes of frost.
A clear day often has the cold bother;
Let me sail on the Bohai Sea uncrossed.

25

七绝
望远
（步韵孟浩然《渡浙江问舟中人》）

一岭陶情两岭风，
山花押日近分同。
空云淡淡淹飞鸟，
共隐心灵烟黛中。

25

A Seven-Character Quatrain
Looking Far
(Following the Rhyme Sequence of Meng Haoran's Poem *Ask the Man in Boat While Acrossing Qiantang River*)

One ridge's style shows Tao's and on the other winds flow;
The hill blossoms block th' sun yet seem alike nearby.
The pale clouds slowly obscure the flying birds nigh;
My heart hides within the smoke with birds flying slow.

26

渔父引
（顾况体）

花落秋头景明。
雨浇夏尾人清。
神如海阔云平。

26

To the Tune of
Yu Fu Yin
(According to Gu Kuang's Style)

When petals drop, it's early fall with a clear scene;
When rain pours at the end of summer, we're serene.
The mind is like the vast sea and clouds calm and clean.

27

七律
诚诗
（新韵）

自在观心话语纯，
菩提光下可怡神。
黑白格劣疏交往，
造化源明识浅深。
横二横一皆是道，
知生知灭且为邻。
阴霾笃有新晴日，
几许清茶通度门。

27

A Seven-Character Octave
One Admonitory Verse
(New Rhyme)

Observing hearts freely, words we speak will be pure;
In the Bodhi's light, our spirit is glad for sure.
Steering clear of those with bad character and low,
The depth of nature's origin and creation, I'd know.
Horizontal or vertical,both are th' true way;
Knowing birth and death, I'm their neighbor anyway.
There'll surely be a sunny day after the haze;
Some cups of tea enlighten me in later days.

28

虞美人
宝黛恋

相随宝黛清风累，
不愿痴心退。
落花泪眼共灵犀，
缱绻红尘虚幻沐春时。

情深缘浅迷魂路，
离散如烟幕。
绛珠仙草了慈恩，
木石前盟挚爱岂容分。

28

To the Tune of
Yu Mei Ren
The Romance of Baoyu and Daiyu

Accompanied, Baoyu and Daiyu are tired in breeze;
They won't retreat from their obsessed love with ease.
Fallen flowers and tearful eyes share a tacit feeling;
In the unreal world of red dust, they enjoy the grace of
spring.

Deep love with shallow fate,they tread on a bewitching
way,
Dispersed like a fading smoke veil today.
Fairy Crimson Pearl has repaid kindness of Spirit Jade;
The true love between the wood and the stone could never
be strayed.

29

蝶恋花
梁祝

草长莺飞春泪绕。
彩蝶双双，寂寞花前耀。
曾许人间情不老，
三生缘定心相照。

穿越千年遗未杳。
惹世悲伤，痛把红尘悼。
雨解英台身死报，
倾盆淋透贞清傲。

29

To the Tune of
Die Lian Hua
The Butterfly Lovers

When grass grows and warblers fly, spring's tears swirl
around.
Pairs of butterflies flit around, in flowers profound.
Once they gave a vow that their love would never age;
The predestined bond of three lives makes hearts engage.

Through thousands of years th' legend of their love
remains,
Causing the world's sadness, mourning the red dust with
pains.
The rain understood Ying Tai's sacrifice with strife,
Pouring down,it soaked through her pure and lofty life.

30

七绝
致救命恩人周万里大夫

生于乡土济人勤，
百卉悉尝灵药分。
曾解疑难无数劫，
愿凭热血抚寒芹。

30

A Seven-Character Quatrain
Ode to Doctor ZHOU Wanli, My Lifesaver

Born in the rural land,you save patients in plight;
Tasting all kinds of plants,you distinguish th' herbs right.
You have saved countless lives from difficult crises;
With warm blood you're willing to relieve the poor quite.

31

七绝
念海外 Sarah

远征东雁赤心魂，
护甲加身为梦奔。
好友当年同起步，
一观云上一屯根。

31

A Seven-Character Quatrain
Missing Ms. Sarah Abroad

Like an eastern goose, you march far with a true heart;
With the armor on, you pursue the dream so fine.
As good friends, in the past along we took our part,
One watches clouds, the other lives at home of mine.

32

五律
清明清吟

窄窄相思扣，
深深素里修。
红尘吹岁襞，
碧血挡坟囚。
清念执衫袂，
纯心化玉钩。
身传何所许，
如缎浴风流。

32

A Five-Character Verse
Chanting on the Qingming Festival

The slender knot of the yearning so blue,
Deeply refined in the profound white hue.
The red dust riffles the wrinkles of years;
The crimson blood still guards the tombs from fears.
My clear thought holds sleeves that are fluttering,
And pure heart forms th' jade hook moon that's shining.
What goal do we live for all our lifetime?
We're like satin, bathing in th' charm of prime.

33

五律
思屈子
（新韵）

幽风葬汝魂，
寂寞几重深。
无道量屈子，
清真证此身。
红尘明月落，
仕路尽棘纷。
心与汨罗去，
浮沉集浪吟。

33

A Five-Character Verse
Thinking About Qu Yuan
(New Rhyme)

Your soul was entombed in the sombre breeze;
You endured so much loneliness back then.
Qu Zi was judged by the rules of the sleaze;
The pureness proved your innocence again.
In the mortal world the moon set at night;
Your official career was all th' rough more.
Your heart went with th' Miluo River on site;
Floating, you gathered the waves' sound for sure.

34

五律
夏日

春心牵五月，
寻处置闲身。
热浪袭门扰，
清风动水氤。
麦熟遥系带，
云卷庶亲民。
浮笔添诗意，
方圆朋辈人。

34

A Five-Character Verse
The Summer Days

The heart of spring brought back to May;
I'm looking for a place to dwell.
Hot waves disturb my door all day;
Light breeze yet makes the river swell.
Ripe wheat afar looks like a belt;
Curled clouds are kind to th' common boor.
With a flighty pen th' verse is spelt,
Which all friends around may adore.

35

西江月
拜访张子立老师

缕缕清风联袂，
白云一路轻飘。
三行姐妹悦眉梢，
不忘恩师慧教。

崇德扎根尚礼，
习文拔节培桃。
劳心一脉映今朝，
唯愿先生安好。

注：三姐妹系同窗刘向荣、桑小红与我。

35

To the Tune of
Xi Jiang Yue
Visiting My Teacher ZHANG Zili

Waves of fresh breeze are blowing together;
White clouds are drifting gently all the way.
The three sisters are so happy and gay,
Never forget dear teacher's guides each day.

You said virtue and manner should take root,
Nurturing talents through writing someway.
Your painstaking efforts reflect today;
That our teacher is well we only pray.

Note: The three sisters refer to my classmates LIU
Xiangrong, SANG Xiaohong and me.

36

如梦令
蝴蝶飞飞来院

蝴蝶飞飞来院，
慕我琴书相伴。
独立小楼旁，
昨种玫瑰一片。
如见，
如见，
遥远故乡浮现。

36

To the Tune of
Ru Meng Ling
Butterflies Fly to My Courtyard

The butterflies fly to my courtyard fine,
Envying my zither an' books which are mine.
I stand alone by the small building,
Here are roses grown before in a line.
I see them fine;
I see them fine;
My distant hometown appears in th' sunshine.

37

清平乐
读《胡宁诗词选集》

方圆书遍，
又把山河赞。
卷里君容青竹伴，
道破晴空浩瀚。

曲赋润比春风，
长襟靓过芙蓉。
上挽白云片片，
下吟夏蝶秋虫。

37

To the Tune of
Qing Ping Yue
Reading the *Selected Poems of HU Ning*

You write everything around you ,

And glorify mountains and rivers too.
In poems your look stays with the verdant bamboo;
You can just reveal the sky vast and blue.

Songs and Odes are as sweet as th' spring breeze there;
Your long skirt is prettier than Lotus fair.
Up you hold the pieces of white clouds and
down chant summer butterflies an' fall bugs rare.

38

清平乐
李正栓教授《毛泽东诗词精华（汉英葡）》悉读有感

气冲霄汉，
笔墨霜花现。
阅尽沧桑生主见，
今日感知美满。

英汉葡语西东，
尽升华夏文明。
万籁依依他日，
春光引路前行。

38

To the Tune of
Qing Ping Yue
Thoughts on Proffesor LI Zhengshuan's *Gems of Mao Zedong's Poems*

With high spirit reaching the sky,
The frost shows in your pen and ink so high.
After reading th' past in poems, wisdom I fly,
Now for thy divine translation I sigh.

Chinese English an' Portuguese, east and west,
Have promoted the Chinese culture best.
All the sounds will linger in the future,
The spring scene leads us forward without rest.

39

阳关曲
中秋节
（新韵）

暖阳流翠近秋深，
欲采斑斓寄远亲。
伴君路上避风雨，
圆月同升明照心。

39

To the Tune of
Yang Guan Qu
On the Mid-Autumn Day
(New Rhyme)

The sunlight shines on green plants near late fall;
I want to pick rich hues for kins afar.
With thee on th' road, we shun rains big and small;
Meanwhile,our hearts are shone by th' full moon far.

40

忆江南
中秋有思

菊花秀，
远望月光柔。
满鬓青丝今雪沤，
青身衣履恰逢秋，
心意柳梢收。

40

To the Tune of
Yi Jiang Nan
My Thought on the Mid-Autumn Festival

Mums display such fair mien;
From afar tender the moon I've seen.
My hair on the temples is dyed snow-white;
Just fit for fall are my shoes and dress green;
My mind flies to the willow tops keen.

41

七律
话梨园

风徐五月点花腔，
竹韵依人上碧妆。
断鼓身羁天下事，
梨园扇议世人章。
旋音流水穿珠璧，
深籁逢云化玉疆。
国运风光君记予，
神州宣处舞霓裳。

41

A Seven-Character Octave
Talking About the Operatic Circle

The tune is even better in the breeze of May;
On stage the lush green bamboos are near actors bright.
The beats of drums remain on unfair things away;
The fans there should assess the people's words wrong or
right.
The whirling sound is like water through walls of beads;
The pleasant sounds rise to clouds, then open green sight.
You should bring honor for our country through your
deeds;
In th' land of China, you dance in fair clothes in flight.

42

七律
临近中秋有感
（新韵）

移面东风挽送秋，
盘庚岁序借云侯。
光阴随季压墙草，
天地为心诚子眸。
试问青山谁锦著？
竟答侪辈各英流。
鹭飞滩淖辞高务，
共我人间一致游。

42

A Seven-Character Octave
My Thoughts Near the Mid-Autumn Festival
(New Rhyme)

Stroking my face the east wind comes with fall;
I count seasons by the change of clouds curled.
In four seasons, the grass changes on the wall;
Earth and sky are th' mind for men to view th' world.
May I ask who adorned the lush green hill?
It's we who tried first to produce scenes fair.
Egrets alight on muddy beach near th' rill,
With me to see worldly things here and there.

43

七律
秋末
（新韵）

喝断秋光共月明，
繁华凋落与西风。
人间增挂菊一盏，
指上携欢柳数青。
香溢农园及藕苑，
雀游屋舍复兰亭。
心堪添处常深记，
半获收成半塑卿。

43

A Seven-Character Ocative
The Late Autumn
(New Rhyme)

I shout fall light to stop and share th' moon bright;
Flowers in full bloom will fade in the wind west.
Th' world is added a lamp-like mum fair quite;
With my glad hands I play with wickers best.
Th' scent comes from lotus garden and farm land;
From the house to the bower the birds fly.
In my heart I often remember, and
Half is for crop, half for you to thrive aye!

44

七律
重阳有寄

人归平淡夏归秋，
弦月携风上小楼。
昔日亲朋遥对岸，
今朝黄叶近荒丘。
东篱寄我茱萸影，
夙愿成歌暖迹畴。
露抱菊残常有泪，
琴书作伴几清流。

44

A Seven-Character Octave
My Emotions on the Double Ninth Festival

Life turns plain as summer is to fall ah!
First quarter moon is up the tower with wind.
The old friends are on the other bank far;
Today brown leaves flew near th' bleak hill we find.
East fence has cornel's shadows in my mind;
My long wish has turned a song with warm deeds.
The dews on the mums oft look like tears shined;
With book and lyre along, it's the life's creeds.

45

七律
重阳有寄
（新韵）

残荷昨夜又腰弯，
假醉清风远玉栏。
独对菊花犁乱绪，
谁依书案辨谬言。
逢人总用长安句，
采意皆凭肺腑言。
鬓雪压眉祈望月，
思亲何在垒心寒。

45

A Seven-Character Octave
My Sentiments on the Double Ninth Festival
(New Rhyme)

The lotus leaves did stoop again last night;
Feignedly drunk, the wind's far from jade rails.
I face mums alone with my mood in plight ;
Who leans against the desk to tell false tales?
When meeting guys, we'll oft say good luck max,
I take the kind advice from someone smart.
My white hair palls brows an' I pray moon to wax;
Missing kith and kin I'm sad in my heart.

46

七绝
落叶竹
（新韵）

雪后冰杀倔强竹，
如人挺立叶萧疏。
筛风望水临书院，
一片清心尘岁除。

46

A Seven-Character Quatrain
Deciduous Bamboos
(New Rhyme)

After snow stubborn bamboos ice did kill;
With few dry leaves they stand upright like men.
Near th' academy they sift wind an' view th' rill,
Making my mind pure an' dusty time gone then.

47

七绝
望海潮

滚滚波涛下九霄，
一轮明日自妖娆。
潮汐曾煮千斤雪，
浪过风华别雾飘。

47

A Seven-Character Quatrain
Viewing the Tide Bore

The mighty waves surge from the heaven;
The bright sun blazes alone in the sky.
The tide boiled up snow of many a ton;
The charm fades in the mist as waves roll by.

48

七绝
与荷书

欲把清风比作亲，
青姿热血碧空吟。
觉疏常盼儿捎语，
几许荷花系夙心。

48

A Seven-Character Quatrain
The Ode to Lotus

Th' wind blows to me as a loved one does come;
The youth's life is sung with blood in clear air.
I can't sleep well an' wish my girl pass words some,
How many lotus tie to my mind there?

49

七绝
致谢李正栓教授赠书

行行文字覆西东，
每蕴知行心血融。
译海青春多奋志，
攀高生气似英鸿。

49

A Seven-Character Quatrain
Thanks to Profesor LI Zhengshuan for Gifting
Me the Book

Lines of words cross countries of East and West,
With your thought an' conduct you' ve made efforts still.
In translation sea you've fought in youth best;
Like a brave swan you climb high with strong will.

50

七绝
晨霁

多朝危雨一朝晴，
忽见清新绿意明。
蜂领黄花扬媚好，
阳光携伴绕云行。

50

A Seven-Character Quatrain
The Scene After the Rain in the Morning

It's clear today after storms for many a day ;
Suddenly seeing fresh and bright green fair I'm gay.
How friendly bees are with the yellow flowers there!
Around the clouds with its close friends walks the sun ray.

51

七绝
霜降
（新韵）

枚枚落叶锁霜魂，
暮色苍茫景色深。
跌进苍茫藏苦骨，
浮烟速染树间尘。

51

A Seven-Character Quatrain
Frost's Descent
(New Rhyme)

All fallen leaves locked the soul of the frost;
At dusk the scenery is very vast.
Fallen in th' vast, hard leaves' spirit is lost;
The smoke dirtied the dust in the trees fast.

52

七绝
小院闲冬

西风拖拽雪花开，
热血兰矜寄素怀。
小院清平闲看柳，
折痕满地遍书斋。

52

A Seven-Character Quatrain
The IdLe Winter in My Yard

The west wind fast drags the snowflakes to fly;
The blood and orchid's trait hold my heart nigh.
In the quiet yard I watch willows around;
Cut twigs are in the study an' on the ground.

53

七绝
见落叶感时光

一季繁华殒落飞，
双眉凝蹙且心违。
严寒冬日园中雪，
必挽春光送驾归。

53

A Seven-Character Quatrain
Sighing Time When I See Leaves Falling Down

Now lush blooms perished an' fallen leaves fly all the way;
My brows knit and my heart is sad for them today.
In the cold winter the snowflakes fall in the park;
They're bound to usher in the vernal breeze one day.

54

七绝
怀念许渊冲先生

先生学问贯东西，
译海融身无倦题。
三美流芳为爱举，
清风青史上云梯。

54

A Seven-Character Quatrain
In Memory of Mr. XU Yuanchong

Your knowledge is famous in th' east and west;
You engaged in translation sans complaint.
Three beauties are worthy of love the best;
Your noble style in the history won't faint.

55

七绝
悼袁隆平和吴孟超院士
（新韵）

苍茫寥廓骤云低，
咽过悲风九域弥。
何讯东君频乱雨，
双星同去锁忧急。

55

A Seven-Character Quatrain
Mourning for Academicians
Yuan Longing and Wu Mengchao
(New Rhyme)

The grey clouds suddenly hung low in the vast sky;
In th' land of China people shed tears in wind aye.
Why did the God of fair spring fall the chaotic rain?
The two stars were gone, so we are all sad in pain.

56

七绝
偶遇蔷薇

一缕清风垣上收，
蔷薇挽臂最英流。
魂飞旭日霞翻早，
解把青春藏玉侯。

56

A Seven-Character Quatrain
Meeting Roses by Chance

A gust of wind rests in front of the wall;
The roses grow and verdant they are all.
The sun shines early in the charming rays,
And leads my heart to hide in youthful days.

57

七绝
思念
（新韵）

遥望天空囚小楼，
几江烟雨为君愁。
迎风把盏频白发，
燕自回家檐下休。

57

A Seven-Character Quatrain
Missing
(New Rhyme)

I sit in the small garret and look at the sky;
A few rivers of misty rains worry for you.
Facing wind, with gray hair I wine in sad mood aye;
The swallows have come home and roost under th' eaves
too.

58

七绝
小花园

馨香入户几垂涎，
驱散幽沉夜幕天。
小院寂然花露冷，
由心郁郁惹人怜。

58

A Seven-Character Quatrain
The Small Garden

I long for th' scent wafting into my room;
It drives out the very gloomy night sky.
In quiet yard the dew is cool on th' bloom,
It made me pine constantly with a sigh.

59

七绝
暑居

今日难寻满地花，
园中唯有柳枝斜。
银藤雨后游廊挂，
聊解心神共看家。

59

A Seven-Character Quatrain
My House in Dog Days

I can not find the flowers everywhere today;
In the park only leaning willow twigs are there.
After rain on the porch hangs honeysuckle fair;
They relax me and watch my house with me someway.

60

七绝
仲夏即景
（新韵）

去年今日此中逢，
满目葱茏读落英。
且看清风愁北咏，
浮云亦妒隐身形。

60

A Seven-Character Quatrain
The Scene in Midsummer
(New Rhyme)

Last year on this day here I met the scene;
Counting fallen blooms, I saw the lush green.
Facing th' breeze I fret for whistling north wind;
So jealous the clouds have hid their own mien.

61

七绝
题老树

一身苍凛到穷年，
把酒邀歌几世欢？
曾与雷公争日月，
蓬头不见少时冠。

61

A Seven-Character Quatrain
Ode to the Old Tree

In dark green you are majestic till you are old;
When did you sing joyfully with the wine you hold?
Once you fought with the Thunder for the moon and sun,
But now your hair is unkempt and youth's hair is none.

62

七绝
初夏之湖

水波凝碧载云天，
疫过芦花缀岸边。
信步盈芳相去久，
清风已上柳湖烟。

62

A Seven-Character Quatrain
The Lake in Early Summer

Waves spray verdant splashes under the sky;
Plagues gone, reed-blooms fringe the shore nearby.
A long walk in th' flower clusters I take;
Breeze lulls the mists over the willow lake.

63

七绝
冬柳

一任寒风寂寞依，
苍凉入目也非题。
曾经拦破春秋雨，
今对芦花负雪犁。

63

A Seven-Character Quatrain
The Winter Willow

No matter how lonely in the cold wind you feel;
What I'll say isn't the wintry scene in a great deal.
You once cut through the spring and fall rains hurriedly;
Today you and reeds work hard in the snow with zeal.

64

七绝
随感

欣将心事许春光，
未伴梅花妆点香。
独到梦中来看雪，
眉边亦挂小冰霜。

64

A Seven-Character Quatrain
My Random Thoughts

I'm glad to give my heart to the spring fine,
Not with plum blooms to scent the makeup nice.
Alone I view the snow in th' dream of mine;
On my brows hang a little frost and ice.

65

七绝
游菩提岛

穿雾登临细雨斜，
浑朦天地却情嘉。
骑洋跨海如飞度，
壮景舒心忘俗差。

65

A Seven-Character Quatrain
Touring The Bodhi Island

Thro the mist we ascend the isle in the rain light;
The world is so hazy but we are in delight.
We span across the vast ocean as if soaring;
In splendid view we're glad, forgetting all the plight.

66

七绝
惜王相军

爱落凡间泣鬼神，
为君凭吊一湖春。
十年出蜀行川色，
血泪难湮吹哨人。

66

A Seven-Character Quatrain
Lament for WANG Xiangjun

Your love fell into the world and made ghosts shed tears;
With the spring of a lake I sadly mourned for you.
Since leaving Sichuan, you've walked on ice for ten years;
The whistler can't be drowned in blood and tears anew.

67

七绝
咏枫

几许相思抱病残，
一腔碧血染枫丹。
浮云易逝寻常事，
独步他乡复自安。

67

A Seven-Character Quatrain
Ode to Maples

Like illness,some lovesickness disables life aye;
Maple leaves are dyed red by hot blood in th' chest.
It is common for floating clouds to drift away;
Alone they'll settle down wherever it is best.

68

七绝
观枫林

集取秋光万丈鲜，
暮含霜露脉相牵。
枫林逐见飞仙子，
缕缕云霞射向天。

68

A Seven-Character Quatrain
Watching the Maple Woods

You have captured the vast brilliance of fall,
With frost and dew at dusk, th' veins entwine all.
Out of the maple woods fly faeries fair;
Wisps of rosy clouds shoot up to the air.

69

七绝
观古建
（新韵）

一排古建守园林，
清代风格气象新。
不见前朝迁腐气，
但留遗戒满乾坤。

69

A Seven-Character Quatrain
Visiting Ancient Buildings
(New Rhyme)

A row of old buildings stands in the park;
The style of the Qing Dynasty looks new.
Sans previous dynasty's pedantic mark,
To the world it has left a lesson true.

70

七绝
秋感

日月已将秋染红，
蓬飞浩荡沐长空。
莲心碧叶观英久，
复对韶华叹世风。

70

A Seven-Character Quatrain
My Sentiment in Autumn

Autumn is dyed red by the sun and moon;
The fleabanes fly neath the blue sky so vast.
The lotus seeds and leaves watch blooms not soon,
And sigh at the ways of times at long last.

71

七绝
秋感
（依韵余新女士诗）
王树达

风清水静伴晴空，
林谧宜人信步丛。
不采叶金藏卷语，
满含秋韵在心中。

71

**A Seven-Character Quatrain
My Sentiment in Autumn
(Following the Rhyming Pattern
Of Ms. Yu Xin's Poem)
By WANG Shuda**

The wind is mild and water calm in the clear sky;
The woods are mute and fair,in bushes as I stroll.
I don't pluck golden leaves and hide them in my scroll;
I am full of the autumn charm in my heart's eye.

72

七绝
霜降吟
（新韵）

静卧不觉寒露滋，
唐风共咏更宜时。
他乡落叶潇潇下，
寂寞人生是短枝。

72

A Seven-Character Quatrain
Chanting on Frostfall
(New Rhyme)

Calm I lie and do not feel more cold dew;
To sing Tang poetry it's more timely quite.
Like rain the leaves in alien land down flew;
The lonely life is like th' short branch in plight.

73

七绝
斋思

案上荷花听雨声，
陈珠滴玉画方成。
随缘修得莲心在，
抱过晨昏落鸟鸣。

73

A Seven-Character Quatrain
Thoughts in My Study

The lotus on the desk hears the rain's sound;
With crystal ink I complete th' painting bound.
By my fate my lotus heart is retained;
Birds twitter at dawn and dusk, unrestrained.

74

七绝
立秋翌日

热浪依然暑未消，
金花藤上淡香飘。
蝉音绕柳说秋事，
直入云天慰寂寥。

74

A Seven-Character quatrain
The Second Day After the Start of Autumn

The summer heat waves are still going on;
The honeysuckles are so fragrant yon.
Cicadas in th' trees speak of fall in tone;
It'll rise straight to clouds to comfort the lone.

75

七绝
朗月
（新韵）

群山幽醉月登台，
万里江河一镜开。
洗净青石铭志远，
乘风逐日引苍怀。

75

A Seven-Character Quatrain
The Bright Moon
(New Rhyme)

so bright a moon shines atop the drunk greenish hills;
Like a mirror,the moon is clear to light long rills.
Slates cleaned with moonlight let me keep my will in
mind;
It'll lead mundane things to chase the sun with the wind.

76

七绝
夏吟

白云溅水鸟沾天，
信路清风接碧前。
日落西山多一事，
心安此地记青莲。

76

A Seven-Character quatrain
Chanting in Summer

The clouds splashed on water as birds reached th' sky;
A random breeze blew toward the green scene.
At sunset, I had a new task to try,
And stayed here, remembering th' lotus clean.

77

五绝
闲云

云在妙高堂，
堪知众小香。
虚空身下事，
足以缉清芳。

77

A Pentasyllabic Quatrain
The Leisurely Clouds

The clouds float above the hall of wonder,
Aware of the scents of all things tender.
The affairs below them are of no care;
They're enough to embrace the fragrant air.

78

五绝
深秋有感

秋风夜色驰，
过客不相知。
梦底听花落，
何人鬓小思?

78

A Pentasyllabic Quatrain
My Feeling in Late Autumn

The autumn wind blows fast at night;
Th' passersby don't mutually know.
In th' dream comes falling blooms' sounds light;
Who hides missing in temples oh?

79

五绝
梅花

冰冷试胸怀，
梅花抱雪开。
暗香侵入骨，
无惧苦寒来。

79

A Pentasyllabic Quatrain
Plum Blossoms

The icy chill yet tests your heart;
The plum blossoms bloom in the snow.
The faint scent pierces into th' bone part;
They fear not bitter cold does flow.

80

五绝
闻诵《沁园春•雪》

听风寒刺破，
蜡舞大江河。
天籁含香远，
吟诗赤县歌。

80

A Pentasyllabic Quatrain
Versing About the Chanting "To the Tune of
Qin Yuan Chun•Snow"

I hear the cold winds pierce the air today;
Over great rivers flurries the snow white.
Th' sounds of nature with scent spreads far away;
We chant poems for our great China bright.

81

五绝
五九

冬寒落日徊，
河畔玉冰开。
回看西风里，
枯枝钓月来。

81

A Pentasyllabic Quatrain
The Fifth Cold Nine Days in Winter

The setting sun lingers in th' winter chill;
The jade-ice melts in the side of the rill.
Looking back I find that in the west wind,
The withered branch is fishing th' moon at will.

82

五绝
立秋

今日清风始，
轻凉散暑忧。
萱花及草木，
一步汇成秋。

82

A Pentasyllabic Quatrain
Beginning of Autumn

Today the soft cool breeze begins to play,
Dispelling summer's heat and care away.
The bright daylilies, grass, and trees so gay,
In just one step merge into autumn's sway.

83

五绝
蜗居

云倦日西驰，
无为赏雀姿。
风传花信语，
复叩小门知。

83

A Pentasyllabic Quatrain
My Humble Abode

The clouds wearied, the sun sets west;
I do naught but enjoy birds' play.
The wind spreads the floral news best,
Knocking at my door all the way.

84

七绝
题长城万里图
（新韵）

鬼道千门万里关，
接天避日护中原。
贫兰胜紫初将尽，
犹似浮云放马宽。

84

A Seven-Character Quatrain
The Painting of The Great Wall of Ten-Thousand Li
(New Rhyme)

On great wall are passes with changing roads and gates;
It protects Central Plains, blocking the sun in th' sky.
The slight blue over purple wanes and ends in straits,
It's like a horse galloping among wide clouds high.

85

七绝
南国晨景

红墙入目爽风飘，
椰树葱枝遮碧宵。
气质清新如浣洗，
心居此地乐逍遥。

85

A Seven-Character Quatrain
The Morning Landscape in the South

In the cool wind th' red walls appear in sight;
Th' lush branches of coco block the blue sky.
Like being washed, th' temperament is bright;
If living here, how I enjoy it aye.

86

七绝
步韵孟教授《夏至湖景》

雨瀑雷鸣遁耳嚣，
彩虹丽日衬丝绦。
连吟蛙鼓欢声紧，
绕遍渠塘慰寂寥。

86

A Seven-Character Quatrain
Following Professor Meng's Poem Rhyme "The Lake Scene in Summer"

The yawp of rain and thunder escapes from our ear;
The willow twigs are set off by rainbows and sun.
Continuously the frogs all croak loudly with fun;
Around the pond the lone is warmed by croaking near.

87

七绝
题曾茜女士诗集出版

三百佳篇是锦章，
诗心皆在卷中藏。
珠玑堪比莲花吐，
际会逢缘笔拓疆。

87

A Seven-Character Quatrain
On the Publication of Ms.Zeng Xi's Poetry Collection

Three hundred poems of yours are works fine;
The poetic heart is hidden in your line.
The pearls of words are like lotus' grace;
When meeting fate, your pen expands the space.

88

七绝
题王相军

翻过山涯碾过坡，
迎风泪尽气如河。
转身几许莲花朵，
尽慕英雄铁骨多。

88

A Seven-Character quatrain
Ode to WANG Xiangjun

You climbed over th' cliffs and rolled over slopes of hill;
In th' wind you dried tears but your vigour's like a rill.
So many lilies appeared when you turned around,
All envied your strength as a hero of strong will.

89

十行百字诗
抒怀

放眼凝眸远眺天空皓月，
全年光景将于岁末拢收。
一首首歌曲是如此轻柔，
让冰冷夜温暖漫过心头。
守长庚知梦短扶摇幻境，
见飞雁消宇际有何追求。
曾见这巷陌簪花藏痕水，
我愿随那大雁极目畅游。
天涯路巫山靓闻说已久，
跨疆域盼相逢扯断清愁。

89

100-word Poem of Ten Lines
My Feelings

In the distance I stared at the moon bright;
Whole year's scene will be closed at th' end of th' year.
The songs one by one I heard are soft quite,
Let the warmth in cold night fill my heart drear.
Sleepless, I watched Venus an' rose to dream there;
Lost in skyline, what will geese quest for plan?
I saw blooms and water stains in th' lane fair;
I wish to tour as far as the geese can.
I've long heard the fine tale of Wu Mountain;
'Cross th' bound I long to meet and ease my pain.

（三）

古诗词英译篇

Part III
English Translations of Classical Chinese Poetry

90

金错刀行
陆游
（宋）

黄金错刀白玉装，
夜穿窗扉出光芒。
丈夫五十功未立，
提刀独立顾八荒。
京华结交尽奇士，
意气相期共生死。
千年史册耻无名，
一片丹心报天子。
尔来从军天汉滨，
南山晓雪玉嶙峋。
呜呼！楚虽三户能亡秦，
岂有堂堂中国空无人！

90

Song of the Gold-adorned Sword
Lu You
(Song Dynasty)

My gold-adorned sword is inlaid with the jade white;
Through the window its light sheds into the dark night.
As a man of fifty years , I've no skillful feat;
Sword in hand, looking round I stood alone with feet.
In the capital we made friends with talents great;
Our vow to live and die along will ne'er retreat.
In the long history I am shamed without great name;
With a loyal heart, for the emperor we aim.
You come to th' Han River to join th' army right now,
Facing jagged Zhongnan hills with jade-like white snow.
Alas! destroy Qin but three households of Chu can,
Could it be in great China there's no able man?

91

摊破浣溪沙
李清照
（宋）

病起萧萧两鬓华，
卧看残月上窗纱。
豆蔻连梢煎熟水，
莫分茶。

枕上诗书闲处好，
门前风景雨来佳。
终日向人多酝藉，
木犀花。

91

To the Tune of
Tan Po Huan Xi Sha
LI Qingzhao
(Song Dynasty)

Since I fell ill I find my thin temples turned white;
Lying I see th' waning moon shine through screens at
night.
I boil th' cardamom with its tips into water,
And can't cook tea aright.

Reading poems against the pillow, I feel free;
The scene before the door in the rain is good quite.
All day long kindly staying with me is nothing
But the cistus so bright.

92

(I/II)
阮郎归
张抡
（宋）

寒来暑往几时休，
　光阴逐水流。
浮云身世两悠悠，
　何劳身外求。

天上月，
　水边楼，
须将一醉酬。
陶然无喜亦无忧，
　人生且自由。

92

(I/II)
To the Tune of
Ruan Lang Gui
ZHANG Lun
(Song Dynasty)

The passing of time has never been still;
The time lapses like th' flowing rill.
The cloud and I, both of us, are free real;
We need not seek fame an' gain at will.

Watching the moon in th' sky,
I'm in th' tower by rill;
To get drunk, let me be freewill.
I am carefree, my joy and grief are nil;
In my life, freedom l'll fulfil.

93

（II/II）
阮郎归
张抡
（宋）

谁言无处避炎光，
　山中有草堂。
安然一枕即仙乡，
　竹风穿户凉。

名不恋，利都忘，
　心闲日自长。
不须辛苦觅琼浆，
　华池神水香。

93

(II/II)
To the Tune of
Ruan Lang Gui
ZHANG Lun
(Song Dynasty)

Who says there's no place to avoid the hot sun light;
In the hills my hut is located on site.
When sleeping safely I fell in th' fairy land quite;
The wind from bamboos cools the hut at night.

I don't love my fame and of all gains I lose sight;
Th' day seems to be long when I'm in delight.
I do not have to seek the nice nectar outright;
Th' divine water in my pool is sweet bright.

94

醉垂鞭

张先

（宋）

双蝶绣罗裙，
东池宴，
初相见。
朱粉不深匀，
闲花淡淡春。

细看诸处好，
人人道，
柳腰身。
昨日乱山昏，
来时衣上云。

94

To The Tune Of
Zui Chui Bian
ZHANG Xian
(Song Dynasty)

In silk skirt with butterflies of a pair,
You first met me at the feast,
Beside the Pool of the East.
You did not make up so heavily there,
Just like a vernal wild flower so fair.

Carefully seen, you are actually swell;
Everyone admired well,
O' your slender waist is so rare.
Did you last night come from th' Wu Mount so quare?
As if your dress wore clouds when you were there.I

95

菩萨蛮
忆郎还上层楼曲
张先
（宋）

忆郎还上层楼曲，
楼前芳草年年绿。
绿似去时袍，
回头风袖飘。
郎袍应已旧，
颜色非长久。
惜恐镜中春，
不如花草新。

95

To the Tune of
Pu Sa Man
Missing My Man, I Step onto the Tower Here
ZHANG Xian
(Song Dynasty)

Missing my man, I step onto the tower here;
The sweet grass before the tower turns green per year.
th' green is like th' gown he wore when he took leave;
When he turned round, the wind blew up his sleeve.
His spick-and-span gown must be old and worn;
The green color might not keep so long yon.
I fear there'll fade my look as spring in glass;
It won't renew as the flowers and grass.

96

蝶恋花
欧阳修
（宋）

画阁归来春又晚。
燕子双飞，
柳软桃花浅。
细雨满天风满院，
愁眉敛尽无人见。

独倚阑干心绪乱。
芳草芊绵，
尚忆江南岸。
风月无情人暗换，
日游如梦空肠断。

96

To the Tune of
Die Lian Hua
OUYANG Xiu
(Song Dynasty)

Back from th' painting house, I find spring's ending again.
The swallows fly in pairs,
Wickers are soft an' peach blooms are almost gone then.
The drizzle fills the sky an' the wind fills the yard when,
Frowning tightly I'm not seen by women and men .

I lean against the rail alone with my mood ill.
The grass is luxuriant,
Th' south bank of the Yangtze River I recall still.
The heartless wind and moon have changed our looks at
will;
Th' past sightseeings like dreams make me heartbroken
real.

97

七绝
惠州一绝
苏轼
（宋）

罗浮山下四时春，
卢橘杨梅次第新。
日啖荔枝三百颗，
不辞长作岭南人。

97

A Seven-Character Quatrain
One of the Superb Scenery in Huizhou
SU Shi
(Song Dynasty)

Under Mt.Luofo It's spring all the year;
Each day lokats an' waxberries are fresh here.
If I ate three hundreds lychees a day;
I'd like to be a Lingnan man for aye.

98

七绝
东栏梨花
苏轼
（宋）

梨花淡白柳深青，
柳絮飞时花满城。
惆怅东栏一株雪，
人生看得几清明？

98

A Seven-Character Quatrain
The Pear Blossoms by the East Fence
SU Shi
(Song Dynasty)

T
The willows are green and pear blooms pale white;
Th' town fills with blooms when catkins take their flight.
I'm sad for the snow-white blooms by th' east fence;
How seldom can I see through the life's light?

99

七绝

东坡

苏轼

（宋）

雨洗东坡月色清，
市人行尽野人行，
莫嫌荦确坡头路，
自爱铿然曳杖声。

99

A Seven-Character Quatrain
The East Slope
SU Shi
(Song Dynasty)

On th' east slope washed by rain th' moonshine is clear;
The townsfolks left, and then th' country folks strolled.
Do not despise the stone path bumpy here;
I love the clanging of th' crutch that I hold.

100

七绝
惠崇春江晚景
苏轼
（宋）

两两归鸿欲破群，
依依还似北归人。
遥知朔漠多风雪，
更待江南半月春。

100

A Seven-Character Quatrain
The Evening Scene on Huichong Spring River
SU Shi
(Song Dynasty)

Pairs of geese are leaving the flock away;
Like homing man they are fain to here stay.
The storm in the desert afar they know,
Still spending half-month spring in the south oh.

101

七绝

纵笔

（其一）

苏轼

（宋）

寂寂东坡一病翁，
白须萧散满霜风。
小儿误喜朱颜在，
一笑那知是酒红。

101

A Seven-Character Quatrain
Writing Freely
(I)
SU Shi
(Song Dynasty)

The lonely old man SU Shi, I am ill;
My stylish beard's like frost, chillingly white.
My little son praises my red cheeks still;
Smiling, I blushed because I am drunk quite.

102

七绝
三月晦日偶题
秦观
（宋）

节物相催各自新，
痴心儿女挽留春。
芳菲歇去何须恨，
夏木阴阴正可人。

102

A Seven-Character Quatrain
An Occasional Poem on the Last Day of March
QIN Guan
(Song Dynasty)

Seasonal things urge to renew each day;
The spoony children wish to let spring stay.
When spring flowers fall you need not be blue;
Th' lush summer grass and trees are lovely too.

103

七绝

示客

陆游

（宋）

桑柘成阴百草香，
缲车声里午风凉。
客来莫说人间事，
且共山林夏日长。

103

A Seven-Character Quatrain
To the Guest
LU You
(Song Dynasty)

Morus and cudrania trees form shades an' weeds are sweet;
In th' sound of reeling wheels th' noon wind is cool sans
heat.
Guest don't speak of the mundane affairs in the world;
In the hill woods,let us enjoy the time so neat.

104

七绝
题青泥市萧寺壁
岳飞
（南宋）

雄气堂堂贯斗牛，
誓将贞节报君仇。
斩除顽恶还车驾，
不问登坛万户侯。

104

A Seven-Character Quatrain
Inscribing on the Wall of Xiao Temple in Green
Mud City
YUE Fei
(the Southern Song Dynasty)

My fierce spirit just soars up to the sky;
I swore to avenge the king loyally.
Once killing all foes, I'll take back the king;
I won't ask for rewards and titles high.

105

七绝
雨中登岳阳楼望君山二首
其一
黄庭坚
（宋）

投荒万死鬓毛斑，
生入瞿塘滟滪关。
未到江南先一笑，
岳阳楼上对君山。

105

A Seven-Character Quatrain
Two Poems of Climbing Yueyang Tower in the
Rain and Looking at Jun Hill
(I)
HUANG Tingjian
(Song Dynasty)

With a near touch I was exiled an' my hair is gray;
Live I'm back from Yanyu Pass of Qutang today.
Before getting to Jiangnan I've a smile at will;
Standing on Yueyang Tower, I can watch Jun hill.

106

七绝
雨中登岳阳楼望君山二首
其二
黄庭坚
（宋）

满川风雨独凭栏，
绾结湘娥十二鬟。
可惜不当湖水面，
银山堆里看青山。

106

A Seven-Character Quatrain
Two Poems of Climbing Yueyang Tower in the
Rain and Looking at Jun Hill
(II)
HUANG Tingjian
(Song Dynasty)

Alone I lean on rails, th' lake is full of wind an' rain;
As fair as Lady Xiang's twelve buns is th' hill scene.
Alas, just on the lake's midst I can't stand fain;
In the silver hills, I behold the mountain green.

107

七绝
和陈君仪读《杨太真外传》
（五首选一）
黄庭坚
（宋）

《梁州》一曲当时事，
记得曾拈玉笛吹。
端正楼空春昼永，
小桃犹学淡胭脂。

107

A Seven-Character Quatrain
Responding to Chen Junyi About Reading
'Lady Yang's Gaiden'
(I/V)
HUANG Tingjian
(Song Dynasty)

When Lady Yang presented a song called "Liangzhou",
People recalled that she picked up th' jade flute to blow.
Duanzheng Building is empty, but spring days are long;
The peaches still imitate the light rouge of beau.

Note: Duan Zheng Building, Yang Guifei's makeup room
in Huaqing Palace.

108

七绝
咏柳
曾巩
（宋）

乱条犹未变初黄，
倚得东风势便狂。
解把飞花蒙日月，
不知天地有清霜。

108

A Seven-Character Quatrain
Remarks on the Willows
ZENG Gong
(Song Dynasty)

The tangled wicker has not yet grown yellow fair;
Relying on th' east wind, to become wild you dare.
You know to cover the sun and moon by catkins,
But don't know between heaven and earth the frost's there.

109

七绝
夏夜追凉
杨万里
（宋）

夜热依然午热同，
开门小立月明中。
竹深树密虫鸣处，
时有微凉不是风。

109

A Seven-Character Quatrain
Seeking the Coolness on a Summer Night
YANG Wanli
(Song Dynasty)

It is as hot as midday in the night;
Opening the door I stand in the moon light.
In deep bamboos and thick woods insects chirp;
Sometimes comes th' cool instead of breeze on site.

110

七绝
初夏
范成大
（宋）

晴丝千尺挽韶光，
百舌无声燕子忙。
永日屋头槐影暗，
微风扇里麦花香。

110

A Seven-Character Quatrain
The Early Summer
FAN Chengda
(Song Dynasty)

The thousand-foot long fine silk strives to make time stay;
Shrikes stop calling but swallows are busy per day.
All day shades of locust trees by the house are dark;
The scent of wheat is fanned in the breeze all the way.

111

七绝
舟下建溪
方惟深
（宋）

客航收浦月黄昏，
野店无灯欲闭门。
倒出岸沙枫半死，
系舟犹有去年痕。

111

A Seven-Character Quatrain
The Boat Sailing to Jian Stream
FANG Weishen
(Song Dynasty)

The vessel reaches the shore in the dim moonlight;
I see th' lampless inn is about to close tonight.
Th' boat's tied to a half dead and bare-rooted maple;
The mark of its mooring last year is still in sight.

112

七绝
山雨
翁卷
（宋）

一夜满林星月白，
亦无云气亦无雷。
平明忽见溪流急，
知是他山落雨来。

112

A Seven-Character Quatrain
Raining in the Hill
WENG Juan
(Song Dynasty)

O'ernight woods were full of star an' moon lights bright;
There're nor cloudy air an' nor thunder last night.
At dawn I see water flow fast in th' rill,
Knowing it's from the rains of yonder hill.

113

小雅

采薇

凯旋而归

（选自《诗经》）

昔我往矣，
杨柳依依。
今我来思，
雨雪霏霏。

行道迟迟，
载渴载饥。
我心伤悲，
莫知我哀！

113

Little Elegance
Picking Vetch
Coming Back After Triumph
(From The Book of Songs)

Then when I went to fight,
Willows were reluctant quite.
Now I'll home in delight,
But snowflakes are in flight.

Th' road is long and I'm slow;
I hunger and thirst, oh!
My heart is full of woe;
The pain of mine none know!

114

绝句
杜甫
（唐）

两个黄鹂鸣翠柳，
一行白鹭上青天。
窗含西岭千秋雪，
门泊东吴万里船。

114

A Quatrain
DU Fu
(Tang Dynasty)

In the green willows two orioles cry;
A line of egrets soar into th' blue sky.
Through th' pane, age-old snow on th' west hill I view;
Before the gate moor ships far from East Wu.

115

七绝
惜牡丹花
白居易
（唐）

惆怅阶前红牡丹，
晚来唯有两枝残。
明朝风起应吹尽，
夜惜衰红把火看。

115

A Seven-Character Quatrain
Cherishing the Peony
BAI Juyi
(Tang Dynasty)

The peonies before steps make me sad;
At dusk two of them left are in bloom bad.
Next morn th' wind would blow off all flowers bright;
With a torch I watch withered ones at night.

116

浪淘沙
借问江潮与海水
白居易
（唐）

借问江潮与海水，
何似君情与妾心。
相恨不如潮有信，
相思始觉海非深。

116

To the Tune of
Lang Tao Sha
May I Ask the River Tide and the Brine
BAI Juyi
(Tang Dynasty)

May I ask the river tide and the brine,
What is his love like and what about mine?
I hate that not tide-punctual is he;
When missing him I know not deep is sea.

237

117

七绝

谒山

李商隐

（唐）

从来系日乏长绳，
水去云回恨不胜。
欲就麻姑买沧海，
一杯春露冷如冰。

117

A Seven-Character Quatrain
Visiting the Mountain
LI Shangyin
(Tang Dynasty)

There is never a long rope to tie the sun still;
The passing rills and drifting clouds are hateful ill.
From the fairy Magu I want to buy the sea,
But there's a cup of spring dew left that's ice-like chill.

118

七绝
相思
王维
（唐）

红豆生南国，
春来发几枝。
愿君多采撷，
此物最相思。

118

A Seven-Character Quatrain
Lovesickness
WANG Wei
(Tang Dynasty)

Ormosia trees grow in south land;
How many twigs will sprout in spring?
I wish you would pick more beans grand,
For th' most lovesickness they could bring.

七绝
秋夜曲
王维
（唐）

桂魄初生秋露微，
轻罗已薄未更衣。
银筝夜久殷勤弄，
心怯空房不忍归。

119

A Seven-Character Quatrain
The Melody of Autumn Night
WANG Wei
(Tang Dynasty)

The moon's up and slight autumn dews beget;
In thin silk dress, she has not changed it yet.
She keeps playing th' silver harp late at night,
To go back to her void room she fears quite.

120

七绝

溪兴

杜荀鹤

（唐）

山雨溪风卷钓丝，
瓦瓯篷底独斟时。
醉来睡着无人唤，
流到前溪也不知。

120

A Seven-Character Quatrain
The Joy in the Stream
DU Xunhe
(Tang Dynasty)

The hill rains and brook winds tangle my fishing line;
With crock alone I sit beneath th' awning and wine.
When I'm drunken and asleep, no one awakes me,
I don't know the boat has floated to th' front creek fine.

121

七绝
同州端午
殷尧藩
（唐）

鹤发垂肩尺许长，
离家三十五端阳。
儿童见说深惊讶，
却问何方是故乡。

121

A Seven-Character Quatrain
The Dragon Boat Festival in Tong Zhou
YIN Yaofan
(Tang Dynasty)

My white hair down to shoulders is a foot long near;
It is the thirty-fifth year since I left home here.
The children are both glad and surprised to hear me,
But they all ask me where my old hometown is, dear.

122

七绝

汉江

杜牧

（唐）

溶溶漾漾白鸥飞，
绿净春深好染衣。
南去北来人自老，
夕阳长送钓船归。

122

A Seven-Character Quatrain
Han River
DU Mu
(Tang Dynasty)

The gentle ripples startle white gulls to take flight;
The green spring seems to dye the clothes charming and
fair.
The people going to and fro will age with care;
The setting sun often sends fishing boats in sight.

123

七绝
塞上听吹笛
高适
（唐）

雪净胡天牧马还，
月明羌笛戍楼间。
借问梅花何处落，
风吹一夜满关山。

123

A Seven-Character Quatrain
Listening to the Flute on the Border
GAO Shi
(Tang Dynasty)

The warriors herd steeds back when the snow is cleared
quite;
They play the fifes in th' watchtower under moon bright.
May I ask where the fine plum blossom tune will fall?
It'll fall all over Guanshan in the wind all night.

124

七绝
檀溪
胡曾
（唐）

三月襄阳绿草齐，
王孙相引到檀溪。
的卢何处埋龙骨，
流水依然绕大堤。

124

A Seven-Character Quatrain
Tanxi Stream
HU Ceng
(Tang Dynasty)

In March Xiangyang's full of weeds green;
The princes tour Tan stream with me.
The Dilu steed's tomb we can't see;
Round the dike still flows the stream clean.

125

七绝
河湟旧卒
张乔
（唐）

少年随将讨河湟，
头白时清返故乡。
十万汉军零落尽，
独吹边曲向残阳。

125

A Seven-Character Quatrain
The Old Soldier in Hehuang War
ZHANG Qiao
(Tang Dynasty)

When young I joined th' army to fight in Hehuang war;
When the border was safe, white-haired I homed afar.
The one hundred thousand soldiers lost their lives near;
To the setting sun 'lone I flute frontier song here.

126

七绝
马诗
（其五）
李贺
（唐）

大漠沙如雪，
燕山月似钩。
何当金络脑，
快走踏清秋。

126

A Seven-Character Quatrain
Steed Poems
(V)
Li He
(Tang Dynasty)

The sand in th' vast desert looks like snow white;
The moon o'er Yan Mts. seems like a hook bright.
When could my steed be harnessed with gold?
My steed galloping in th' clear fall is bold.

127

七绝
南园十三首
其一
李贺
（唐）

花枝草蔓眼中开，
小白长红越女腮。
可怜日暮嫣香落，
嫁与春风不用媒。

127

A Seven-Character Quatrain
Thirteen Poems of the South Garden
(I)
LI He
(Tang Dynasty)

The sprays and vines are blooming in my sight;
They're like Xi Shi's cheeks more red and less white.
'Tis a pity, sweet flowers fell at dusk;
They wed th' spring wind sans matchmaker on site.

128

七绝
南园十三首
其二
李贺
（唐）

宫北田塍晓气酣，
黄桑饮露窣宫帘。
长腰健妇偷攀折，
将餧吴王八茧蚕。

128

A Seven-Character Quatrain
Thirteen Poems of the South Garden
(II)
LI He
(Tang Dynasty)

In fields north of the Palace the dawn mist is thick;
Rustling,the palace drapes th' dewy mulberries flick.
A big woman climbs th' tree for leaves on the sly here,
To feed silkworms of Wu that's ripe eight times a year.

129

七绝
南园十三首
其三
李贺
（唐）

竹里缲丝挑网车，
青蝉独噪日光斜。
桃胶迎夏香琥珀，
自课越佣能种瓜。

129

A Seven-Character Quatrain
Thirteen Poems of the South Garden
(III)
LI He
(Tang Dynasty)

In th' bamboos they reel silk wi' a spinning wheel at will,
Till the sun slants west, green cicadas alone shrill.
Like amber th' peach gum gives off scent to greet summer;
I myself teach th' Yue servants to sow melons still.

130

七绝
南园十三首
其四
李贺
（唐）

三十未有二十余，
白日长饥小甲蔬。
桥头长老相哀念，
因遗戎韬一卷书。

130

A Seven-Character Quatrain
Thirteen Poems of the South Garden
(IV)
LI He
(Tang Dynasty)

I'm not yet thirty, but over twenty today;
Often hungry, I live on the potherbs all day.
An old person on the bridge took pity on me,
And gave me a book on military strategy.

131

七绝
南园十三首
其五
李贺
（唐）

男儿何不带吴钩，
收取关山五十州。
请君暂上凌烟阁，
若个书生万户侯？

131

A Seven-Character Quatrain
Thirteen Poems of the South Garden
(V)
LI He
(Tang Dynasty)

Why don't you a manly man carry th' spear
To retrieve th' fifty states of Guanshan hill?
Please step onto th' Lingyan Pavilion here
To see which scholar's th' high official real.

132

七绝
南园十三首
其六
李贺
（唐）

寻章摘句老雕虫，
晓月当帘挂玉弓。
不见年年辽海上，
文章何处哭秋风。

132

A Seven-Character Quatrain
Thirteen Poems of the South Garden
(VI)
LI He
(Tang Dynasty)

I seek passages and choose phrases which are free,
Till the jade-bow moon, against the drape, hangs at dawn.
Every year, can't you see the wars on the Liao Sea?
Where would this verse about sad fall be used thereon?

133

七绝
南园十三首
其七
李贺
（唐）

长卿牢落悲空舍，
曼倩诙谐取自容。
见买若耶溪水剑，
明朝归去事猿公。

133

A Seven-Character Quatrain
Thirteen Poems of the South Garden
(VII)
LI He
(Tang Dynasty)

In the void house, Sima Xiangru sadly sang still;
Dongfang Shuo gained th' king's mercy with his witty skill.
I want to buy a sword from Ruoye Creek some day;
Next day, learn Kung Fu from lords like Mr. Yuan, I will.

134

七绝
南园十三首
其八
李贺
（唐）

春水初生乳燕飞，
黄蜂小尾扑花归。
窗含远色通书幌，
鱼拥香钩近石矶。

134

A Seven-Character Quatrain
Thirteen Poems of the South Garden
(VIII)
LI He
(Tang Dynasty)

The young swallows fly above the rising spring rill;
Gathering the flowers the small-tailed wasps back fly.
Through th' window, far scenes are shown on th' study
drape still;
Biting the bait, the fish is pulled up to th' rock high.

135

七绝
南园十三首
其九
李贺
（唐）

泉沙软卧鸳鸯暖，
曲岸回篙舴艋迟。
泻酒木栏椒叶盖，
病容扶起种菱丝。

135

A Seven-Character Quatrain
Thirteen Poems of the South Garden
(IX)
LI He
(Tang Dynasty)

Mandarin ducks lie on the warm soft sand by th' spring;
Along th' curved shore, a boat is poled and slow moving.
Lifting th' lid of chile leaves,I pour Magnolia wine;
Drunk I hold up th' sick body 'nd plant silk-caltrops fine.

136

七绝
南园十三首
其十
李贺
（唐）

边让今朝忆蔡邕，
无心裁曲卧春风。
舍南有竹堪书字，
老去溪头作钓翁。

136

A Seven-Character Quatrain
Thirteen Poems of the South Garden
(X)
LI He
(Tang Dynasty)

I'm like Bian Rang who recalled Cai Yong today;
Not in the mood for tunes, I lie in the spring breeze.
Here write with the bamboo south of the house I may;
When old, by the creek I'll be a fisher at ease.

137

七绝
南园十三首
其十一
李贺
（唐）

长峦谷口倚嵇家，
白昼千峰老翠华。
自履藤鞋收石蜜，
手牵苔絮长莼花。

137

A Seven-Character Quatrain
Thirteen Poems of the South Garden
(XI)
LI He
(Tang Dynasty)

Ji Kang's home lied at th' mouth of a dale in long hills;
Th' thousand peaks are older than kings in broad daylight.
In rattan shoes I get cliff honey with the thrills;
As I pull water shield, th' moss grows on my hand white.

138

七绝
南园十三首
其十二
李贺
（唐）

松溪黑水新龙卵，
桂洞生硝旧马牙。
谁遣虞卿裁道帔，
轻绡一匹染朝霞。

138

A Seven-Character Quatrain
Thirteen Poems of the South Garden
(XII)
LI He
(Tang Dynasty)

New dragon eggs show in th' black water of Pine Creek;
Old horse tooth-nitrates are nitres that in Gui Cave grew.
Who sent Yu Xin to cut a Taoist robe unique;
Th' stuff is made of a soft silk dyed with th' sunglow hue.

Note: Yu Qing, whose given name was Xin.

139

五律
南园十三首
其十三
李贺
（唐）

小树开朝径，
长茸湿夜烟。
柳花惊雪浦，
麦雨涨溪田。
古刹疏钟度，
遥岚破月悬。
沙头敲石火，
烧竹照渔船。

139

A Five-Character Octave
Thirteen Poems of the South Garden
(XIII)
LI He
(Tang Dynasty)

A path in woods brightened in the morn light;
The tender weeds were wet with mist at night.
Stunning me are snow-like catkins by th' rilll;
By th' stream, the wheat fields a spring rain doth fill.
From the old temple a slow bell comes here;
In hazy hills far hangs th' waning moon blear.
Fishers knock stones to make fire on th' beach,
Kindling bamboos to light fishing boat each.

140

浣溪沙
夏日
善住
（元）

帘卷薰风夏日长，
幽庭脉脉橘花香。
闲看稚子引鸳鸯。

四月雨凉思御夹，
三吴麦秀欲移秧。
不知身在水云乡。

140

To the Tune of
Huan Xi Sha
Summer Day
SHAN Zhu
(Yuan Dynasty)

In long summer when I roll up th' screen th' breeze strokes
me;
In the quiet yard th' scent of orange blooms floats free.
The child leads the mandarin ducks, I idly see.

In the cool April rain, I miss the lined jacket;
In Three Wu land, wheat blooms and rice they will
transplant.
I'm in th' water and clouds country,yet know I can't.

141

咏雪竹
朱元璋
（明）

雪压枝头低，
虽低不着泥。
一朝红日出，
依旧与天齐。

141

A Quatrain
Ode to the Bamboos in the Snow
ZHU Yuanzhang
(Ming Dynasty)

The branches are pressed low by snow;
They can't reach the mud although low.
One day when the red sun comes out,
They'll still stand to the sky straight so.

142

山中雪后
郑燮
（清）

晨起开门雪满山，
雪晴云淡日光寒。
檐流未滴梅花冻，
一种清孤不等闲。

142

A Quatrain
After the Snow in the Mountains
Zheng Xie
(Qing Dynasty)

At dawn I open th' door and see hills full of snow ;
Clear with pale clouds after snow, th' sunshine is cold
so .
The snow on eaves and plum blossoms has not melted
;
Such a sort of lorn scene is an unusual show.

（四）
英诗汉译篇

Part IV
Chinese Translation
of English Poetry

143

The Road Not Taken
Robert Frost (US)

Two roads diverged in a yellow wood,
And sorry I could not travel both
And be one traveler, long I stood
And looked down one as far as I could
To where it bent in the undergrowth;

Then took the other, as just as fair,
And having perhaps the better claim,
Because it was grassy and wanted wear;
Though as for that the passing there
Had worn them really about the same,

And both that morning equally lay
In leaves no step had trodden black.
Oh, I kept the first for another day!
Yet knowing how way leads on to way,
I doubted if I should ever come back.

143

未选之路
罗伯特·弗罗斯特（美）

黄色林中双路分，
可惜不允俱游临。
身为旅者久时立，
眸览其一至远伸。
直到灌丛弯转处，

而择另道美舒心。
身行或有好说法，
草茂多无旧印痕。
尽管对于经那路，
着实踩后感同真。

清晨两个并排列，
落叶足痕未踏陈。
首路唯留他日顾，
两条交错共情存。
吾疑能否折返去，

I shall be telling this with a sigh
Somewhere ages and ages hence:
Two roads diverged in a wood, and I—
I took the one less traveled by,
And that has made all the difference.

吾叹奈何诉此闻。
岁月蹉跎于某地，
树林交汇各途津。
客稀我取此之道，
已塑不同命运人。

144

Looking for a Sunset Bird in Winter
Robert Frost (US)

The west was getting out of gold,
The breath of air had died of cold,
When shoeing home across the white,
I thought I saw a bird alight.

In summer when I passed the place
I had to stop and lift my face;
A bird with an angelic gift
Was singing in it sweet and swift.

No bird was singing in it now.
A single leaf was on a bough,
And that was all there was to see
In going twice around the tree.

144

冬寻落日鸟(绝句五首)
罗伯特·弗罗斯特（美）

西边渐褪晚金黄，
寒彻呼吸已冻僵，
漫步回家穿雪过，
思觉飞鸟落前方。

夏季曾经行此处，
驻足且把脸儿扬，
　鸟名天赋实殊妙
甜美清音鸣啭长。

当下皆无啼漫唱，
独枚叶子挂枝旁，
　徘徊此树两圈看
其乃唯一入目央。

From my advantage on a hill
I judged that such a crystal chill
Was only adding frost to snow
As gilt to gold that wouldn't show.

A brush had left a crooked stroke
Of what was either cloud or smoke
From north to south across the blue;
A piercing little star was through.

站在山巅优势位
吾猜此刻酷寒藏
如同霜落雪花里
金上贴金失耀光。

画笔涂出弯划迹
或为云彩或烟裳
南来北往碧空过，
穿刺小星飘宇苍。

145

Fire and Ice
Robert Frost (US)

Some say the world will end in fire,
Some say in ice.
From what I've tasted of desire
I hold with those who favour fire.
But if it had to perish twice,
I think I know enough of hate
To say that for destruction ice
Is also great
And would suffice.

145

火与冰
罗伯特·弗罗斯特（美）

有人说世界将毁灭于火，
有人说世界将毁灭于冰。
凭我对欲望的体验来说
我赞同那些偏袒火的言说。
但如果世界要消亡两次，
我想我了解足够怨恨
说冰的破坏力亦极大
足够毁灭世界。

146

To LI Po and TU Fu
W.J.B.Fletcher (UK)

Li Po and Tu Fu, pardon that I come,
Lone Nature's pilgrim from a foreign shore.
With you across the misty hills to roam
And see the dragons carry you once more
To peaks aflame with sunset ; to adore
In Nature's shrine, as ye were wont of yore
To see the Iris ride the torrent's foam,
And ruins where high mansions stood before,
The moonbeams glinting on the broken dome,
While some shrill fute the fallen time deplore
Forgive the humble heart and feeble thought,
The faltering fingers that the echo wrought
Of your sweet woodland lore!

146

访古李杜
W.J.B 弗莱彻（英）

诼吾独访二诗仙，
跨岸焚香祭上天。
越岭翻山随雾荡，
驾龙登顶覆夕燃。
曾牵观景玉皇庙，
复看骑涛仙子颜，
凭吊荒墟雄殿宇，
辉明碎顶月光弦。
笛声尖利悲昔往，
感觉卑微望海涵。
十指微微开颤栗，
文甜李杜响林间。

The Eagle
Alfred Lord Tennyson (UK)

HE clasps the crag with crooked hands;
Close to the sun in lonely lands,
Ringed with the azure world, he stands.
The wrinkled sea beneath him crawls;
He watches from his mountain walls,
And like a thunderbolt he falls.

147

浣溪沙
鹰
（中华新韵）
阿尔弗雷德·丁尼生（英）

利爪弯弯扣壁岩，
独居近日可接天，
立于世界抱晶蓝。

身下海波爬浪漫，
山高鹰目注时牵，
疾如雷电落平川。

148

Crossing the Bar
Alfred Lord Tennyson (UK)

Sunset and evening star,
And one clear call for me!
And may there be no moaning of the bar,
When I put out to sea,

But such a tide as moving seems asleep,
Too full for sound and foam,
When that which drew from out the boundless deep
Turns again home.

Twilight and evening bell,
And after that the dark!
And may there be no sadness of farewell,
When I embark;

For though from out our bourne of Time and Place
The flood may bear me far,
I hope to see my Pilot face to face
When I have crossed the bar.

148

渡沙洲
阿尔弗雷德•丁尼生（英）
（四绝句）

日落晚星辉，
清音唤我催。
及吾出海后，
沙地莫伤悲。

潮水若眠寂，
满盈声沫微，
其皆发海底，
今复故乡回。

暮色晚钟唱，
继之暗夜黑。
登船锚起步，
无痛告别归。

缘自时空界，
洪涛漂远身，
沙洲穿越后，
期见领航人。

149

The Miller's Daughter
Alfred Lord Tennyson (UK)

It is the miller's daughter,
And she is grown so dear, so dear,
That I would be the jewel
That trembles at her ear:
For hid in ringlets day and night,
I'd touch her neck so warm and white.

And I would be the girdle
About her dainty dainty waist,
And her heart would beat against me
In sorrow and in rest:
And I should know if it beat right,
I'd clasp it round so close and tight.

149

磨坊主之女
阿尔弗雷德·丁尼生（英）
（3 绝句+3 对句）

伊乃磨坊主至亲，
风姿妩媚动人心。
吾求化作丽珠宝，
颤抖微摇两耳唇。
日夜藏伏伊发鬓，
轻扶玉颈意温存。

吾将化作纤腰带，
环束伊之细柳身。
心跳随伊贴近我，
忧伤律跃境堪分。
心搏安好当知尽，
紧扣相拥情愈深。

And I would be the necklace,
And all day long to fall and rise
Upon her balmy bosom,
With her laughter or her sighs:
And I would lie so light, so light,
I scarce should be unclasp'd at night.

吾愿成为肩上链，
随之起落伴晨昏，
流连美丽酥胸上，
陪伴欢颜与叹音。
吾欲轻盈不舍君，
穿行长夜梦牵魂。

150

Break, Break, Break
Alfred Tennyson (UK)

Break, break, break,
On thy cold gray stones, O Sea!
And I would that my tongue could utter
The thoughts that arise in me.

O, well for the fisherman's boy,
That he shouts with his sister at play!
O, well for the sailor lad,
That he sings in his boat on the bay!

And the stately ships go on
To their haven under the hill;
But O for the touch of a vanish'd hand,
And the sound of a voice that is still!

Break, break, break,
At the foot of thy crags, O Sea!
But the tender grace of a day that is dead
Will never come back to me.

150

破碎，破碎，破碎
阿尔弗雷德·丁尼生（英）

破碎，破碎，破碎，
打在灰色僵冷的礁石上，大海！
我多希望我的喉舌能诉出
我心中涌现的思想。

啊，那渔夫之子多么快乐，
和他的妹妹玩耍着叫嚷！
啊，那少年的水手多美好，
在港湾的小船里引吭高唱！

宏伟的船只庄严向前，
驶向那山脚下的港湾；
但那只消失的手的触摸，
和声音早已消散！

破碎，破碎，破碎，
摔打在峭壁的脚下，大海！
那逝去日子的温情优雅
永不会再回到我身边。

151

The Lake Isle of Innisfree
William Butler Yeats (Ireland)

I will arise and go now, and go to Innisfree,
And a small cabin build there, of clay and wattles
made;
Nine bean rows will I have there, a hive for the
honeybee,
And live alone in the bee-loud glade.

And I shall have some peace there, for peace comes
dropping slow,
Dropping from the veils of the morning to where the
cricket sings;
There midnight's all a-glimmer, and noon a purple
glow,
And evening full of the linnet's wings.

I will arise and go now, for always night and day
I hear the water lapping with low sounds by the shore;
While I stand on the roadway, or on the pavements
gray,
I hear it in the deep heart's core.

151

茵尼斯弗利湖岛
威廉•巴特勒•叶芝（爱尔兰）

起身即去茵尼岛，
编条黏土筑小巢。
芸豆九行蜂一房，
林间独住嗡声高。

穿开晨雾安宁落，
蛐蛐鸣叫唱声嘹。
紫午半夜光迷离，
黄昏到处雀翅飘。

起身即去斯弗岛，
堪闻岸边轻拍涛。
吾立马路人行道，
内心深处响其潮。

152

The White Birds
William Butler Yeats(Ireland)

I would that we were, my beloved, white birds on the
foam of the sea:
We tire of the flame of the meteor, before it can pass by
and flee;
And the flame of the blue star of twilight, hung low on
the rim of the sky,
Has awaked in our hearts, my beloved, a sadness that
never may die.

A weariness comes from those dreamers, dew-dabbled,
the lily and rose,
Ah, dream not of them, my beloved, the flame of the
meteor that goes,
Or the flame of the blue star that lingers hung low in
the fall of the dew:
For I would we were changed to white birds on the
wandering foam—I and you.

I am haunted by numberless islands, and many a
Danaan shore,
Where Time would surely forget us, and Sorrow come
near us no more:
Soon far from the rose and the lily, the fret of the
flames, would we be,
Were we only white birds, my beloved, buoyed out on
the foam of the sea.

152

白鸟
威廉·巴特勒·叶芝（爱尔兰）

亲爱的，愿我们是浪花上白鸟，
厌倦流星闪过逃走前的闪耀。
黄昏时低悬天边的蓝星火光，
唤醒我们心中从未死的哀伤。

倦意来自梦者，露湿百合玫瑰，
啊，亲爱的，可别梦流星的光辉，
或者蓝星火焰在滴露中低徊，
但愿我们化成那白鸟浪尖飞。

我心绕无数海岛和丹尼湖滨，
那儿光阴遗忘人，烦恼不复临。
转眼远离百合玫瑰流星之惑，
只两只白鸟，亲爱的，浮在浪波。

153

The Tiger
William Blake (UK)

Tiger, tiger, burning bright
In the forests of the night,
What immortal hand or eye
Could frame thy fearful symmetry?

In what distant deeps or skies
Burnt the fire of thine eyes?
On what wings dare he aspire?
What the hand dare seize the fire?

And what shoulder and what art
Could twist the sinews of thy heart?
And when thy heart began to beat,
What dread hand and what dread feet?

What the hammer? what the chain?
In what furnace was thy brain?
What the anvil? What dread grasp
Dare its deadly terrors clasp?

153

老虎
威廉·布莱克（英）

老虎通身似火煌，
时当夜晚树林藏。
如何天眼及神手，
翻作非凡匀称妆？

眼射火苗如烈焰，
其出远海或穹苍。
什么翅膀堪其乘，
何样手心敢火尝。

怎样双肩和技艺，
形弯肌腱自心房。
每当心脏始搏动，
即有手足继恐张？

何选铁锤和铁链，
捶出大脑在炉膛？
铁砧什样堪抓握，
恐惧死亡之扣殇？

When the stars threw down their spears,
And water'd heaven with their tears,
Did He smile His work to see?
Did He who made the lamb make thee?

Tiger, tiger, burning bright
In the forests of the night,
What immortal hand or eye
Dare frame thy fearful symmetry?

抛下星光赛矛戟，
清浇眼泪润天堂。
其含微笑对杰作？
其塑尔身和小羊？

老虎通身似火煌，
时值夜晚暗林藏。
如何天眼和神手，
敢塑非凡匀称妆？

154

A Poison Tree
William Blake (UK)

I was angry with my friend;
I told my wrath, my wrath did end.
I was angry with my foe;
I told it not, my wrath did grow.

And I waterd it in fears,
Night & morning with my tears;
And I sunned it with smiles,
And with soft deceitful wiles.

And it grew both day and night,
Till it bore an apple bright.
And my foe beheld it shine,
And he knew that it was mine.

And into my garden stole,
When the night had veild the pole;
In the morning glad I see;
My foe outstretched beneath the tree.

154

毒果树
威廉·布莱克（英）

吾向友嗔怒，
道出气即消。
对敌生愤怒，
无语恨愈高。

恐惧泪浇灌，
朝夕心郁糟。
微笑映之亮，
巧计哄其娇。

日夜均生长，
直至靓果瞧。
敌人观耀闪，
知主乃吾劳。

黑夜指不见，
小偷园内剽。
清晨喜树下，
敌脚仰天朝。

155

All for Love
Lord G. G. Byron (UK)

O talk not to me of a name great in story;
The days of our youth are the days of our glory;
And the myrtle and ivy of sweet two-and-twenty
Are worth all your laurels, though ever so plenty.

What are garlands and crowns to the brow that is
wrinkled?
'Tis but as a dead flower with May-dew besprinkled:
Then away with all such from the head that is hoary—
—
What care I for the wreaths that can only give glory?

O Fame! ——if I e'er took delight in thy praises,
'Twas less for the sake of thy high-sounding phrases,
Than to see the bright eyes of the dear one discover
She thought that I was not unworthy to love her.

There chiefly I sought thee, there only I found thee;
Her glance was the best of the rays that surround thee;
When it sparkled o'er aught that was bright in my story,
I knew it was love, and I felt it was glory.

155

一切为了爱
乔治·戈登·拜伦（英）

休言故事中伟名，
青春美誉是一同。
妙龄多莲常青藤，
足值恁多荣号称。

覆顶花冠压额皱？
恰似枯红玉露就。
苍头白发弃冠去，
何恋光环徒盛誉？

若吾曾喜汝褒奖，
绝非陶醉迷高腔，
而见宝贝明眸闪，
觉我值得情相伴。

多因寻爱唯见卿，
眸光最美绕君行。
吾之故事光彩间，
而知爱临满心欢。

156

She Walks in Beauty
Lord G. G. Byron (UK)

She walks in beauty, like the night
Of cloudless climes and starry skies,
And all that's best of dark and bright
Meet in her aspect and her eyes,
Thus mellowed to that tender light
Which heaven to gaudy day denies.

One shade the more, one ray the less,
Had half impair'd the nameless grace
Which waves in every raven tress
Or softly lightens o'er her face,
Where thoughts serenely sweet express
How pure, how dear their dwelling-place.

And on that cheek, and o'er that brow
So soft, so calm, yet eloquent,
The smiles that win, the tints that glow
But tell of days in goodness spent,
A mind at peace with all below,
A heart whose love is innocent.

156

伊人倩影
乔治·戈登·拜伦（英）

伊人幽步美婷淑，
似夜无云星尽铺。
明暗之中绝美色，
颜眸于此汇娇殊。
此般深刻柔光里，
天国即令华昼无。

阴影多时光渐少，
无名优雅半损涂。
青丝绺绺如漪浪，
颊上幽幽似亮酥。
甜蜜宁思堪流露，
心灵栖处纯净坞。

额眉拂过容呈好，
温柔安静口吐珠。
夺目光华迷魅笑，
行慈多日诉其途。
平和不与它争议，
爱慕天真惠质读。

157

When We Two Parted
Lord G. G. Byron (UK)

When we two parted
In silence and tears,
Half broken-hearted,
To sever for years,
Pale grew thy cheek and cold,
Colder thy kiss;
Truly that hour foretold
Sorrow to this!

The dew of the morning
Sunk chill on my brow;
It felt like the warning
Of what I feel now.
Thy vows are all broken,
And light is thy fame:
I hear thy name spoken
And share in its shame.

157

当我们分别时
乔治·戈登·拜伦（英）

你我分别各西东
默默无言两眼朦，
痛彻已致心欲碎，
天涯伴随数年景。
尔容凝霜失颜色，
汝吻愈发寒如冰。
诚然那刻先兆起
悲哀之情此中生。

清晨珠露浸凉意
寒气落眉添冷星。
它在仿佛警示我，
忧愁恍若与此同。
山盟海誓汝丢弃，
身堕毁誉肆意行。
吾闻汝名遭人讲，
心蒙羞耻无地容。

They name thee before me,
A knell to mine ear;
A shudder comes o'er me--
Why wert thou so dear?
They know not I knew thee
Who knew thee so well:
Long, long shall I rue thee
Too deeply to tell.

In secret we met:
In silence I grieve
That thy heart could forget,
Thy spirit deceive.
If I should meet thee
After long years,
How should I greet thee? --
With silence and tears.

于吾面前提尔姓，
耳畔丧钟即轰鸣。
浑身发抖如战栗，
汝初何故恁衷情？
　人们不晓我识你
境况颇熟深谙卿。
日久之后将汝恨，
恨深恨今闭口声。

你我暗地常幽会，
　今泣无言涕泪零
汝心岂能将吾忘，
汝意何堪骗人情。
　多年以后时光转
或许彼时汝吾逢。
吾应如何称呼你？
无言默默泪眼朦。

158

A girl
Ezra Pound (US)

The tree has entered my hands,
The sap has ascended my arms,
The tree has grown in my breast-
Downward,
The branches grow out of me, like arms.

Tree you are,
Moss you are,
You are violets with wind above them.
A child - so high - you are,
And all this is folly to the world.

158

女孩
埃兹拉·庞德（美）

树融入我的手掌，
汁液漫上我的臂膀，
树长进我胸膛——
向下生长，
枝干延伸出我的躯体，宛如胳膊一样。

绿树是你，
青苔是你，
你是紫罗兰，风儿在头上轻扬。
你和孩童一样娇小，
而这一切对于世界皆是痴妄。

159

Salutation
Ezra Pound (US)

O generation of the thoroughly smug and thoroughly
uncomfortable,
I have seen fishermen picnicking in the sun,
I have seen them with untidy families,
I have seen their smiles full of teeth
and heard ungainly laughter.
And I am happier than you are,
And they were happier than I am;
And the fish swim in the lake
and do not even own clothing.

159

致意
埃兹拉·庞德（美）

自负绝顶一代人，
而感不适烦忧侵。
烈日凌空餐食享，
渔翁家眷垢染身。
余观莞尔齿犹露，
开怀纵笑莽音闻。
吾乐胜汝感不禁，
他们福分胜吾欣。
鱼在湖中逍遥爽，
来去无着摇赤鳞。

160

A Psalm of Life
-----What the heart of the young man said to the psalmist
Henry • Wadsworth • Longfellow (US)

Tell me not, in mournful numbers,
Life is but an empty dream!--
For the soul is dead that slumbers,
And things are not what they seem.

Life is real! Life is earnest!
And the grave is not its goal;
Dust thou art, to dust returnest,
Was not spoken of the soul.

Not enjoyment, and not sorrow,
Is our destined end or way;
But to act, that each to-morrow
Find us farther than to-day.

Art is long, and time is fleeting,
And our hearts, though stout and brave,
Still, like muffled drums, are beating
Funeral marches to the grave.

160

人生颂
——青年心声诗颂
亨利•沃兹沃斯•费朗罗（美）

勿唱哀诗与我听，
徒留空梦付一生。
灵魂沉睡浑然死，
世事难分表里清。

真诚生活非幻境，
孤独坟冢岂达穷。
君为尘土需归去，
斯指精神未化冥。

不论悲伤和乐趣，
而非目的并途程。
赋于实践前方远
发现明朝进步重。

智慧无涯时易逝，
吾侪勇毅胆长萦。
也如闷鼓承捶力
仍对坟莹奏曲鸣。

In the world's broad field of battle,
In the bivouac of Life,
Be not like dumb, driven cattle!
Be a hero in the strife!

Trust no future, howe'er pleasant!
Let the dead Past bury its dead!
Act,--act in the living Present!
Heart within, and God o'erhead!

Lives of great men all remind us
We can make our lives sublime,
And departing, leave behind us
Footprints on the sands of time;

Footprints, that perhaps another,
Sailing o'er life's solemn main,
A forlorn and shipwrecked brother,
Seeing, shall take heart again.

Let us, then, be up and doing,
With a heart for any fate;
Still achieving, still pursuing,
Learn to labor and to wait.

世界茫茫争战场，
露营漠漠寄身丁。
忌当哑畜凭驱往！
要作英雄立马行！

莫望未来多美好！
已亡过去必消融！
活于当下知行早！
对内信心天佑成！

比照伟人识自己
定能高尚败平庸。
转身离去回眸里，
时光漠野足迹从。

也许另足开异路，
亦曾威海泛舟踪。
船翻苦厄一兄在，
眼见遗痕英气升。

唤起精神加倍干，
伴随命运用心耕。
坚持理想和实现，
学会耘田等善成。

161

Bright Star
John Keats (UK)

Bright star, would I were steadfast as thou art---
Not in lone splendour hung aloft the night,
And Watching, with eternal lids apart,
Like nature's patient, sleepless Eremite,

The moving waters at their priestlike task
Of pure ablution round earth's human shores,
Or gazing on the new soft-fallen mask
Of snow upon the mountains and the moors---

No-yet still steadfast, still unchangeable,
Pillow'd upon my fair love's ripening breast,
To feel for ever its soft fall and swell,
Awake for ever in a sweet unrest;

Still, still to hear her tender-taken breath,
And so live ever---or else swoon to death.

161

明亮的星
约翰·济慈（英）

愿吾坚毅似亮星，
不独辉煌挂夜空。
眼眸常睁永观景，
无眠隐士耐心同。

净体祭司流水出，
洗礼人类海岸所。
或者凝视新罩铺，
雪盖群山与荒落。

仍然坚定吾不变，
枕于吾爱之暖胸，
永感温柔起伏间，
甜蜜不安永清醒。

静静听伊轻呼吸，
如此生活或昏死。

162

Love's Witness
Aphra Behn (UK)

Slight unpremeditated Words are borne
By every common Wind into the Air;
Carelessly utter'd, die as soon as born,
And in one instant give both Hope and Fear:
Breathing all Contraries with the same Wind
According to the Caprice of the Mind.

But Billetdoux are constant Witnesses,
Substantial Records to Eternity;
Just Evidences, who the Truth confess,
On which the Lover safely may rely;
They're serious Thoughts, digested and resolv'd;
And last, when Words are into Clouds devolv'd.

162

爱的见证
阿芙拉·贝恩（英）

偶然迷离间轻言的话语，
随寻常气息化成那空气；
恣意一出口旋即随风去，
希望和忧怯袭人不分离；
同样呼吸呼出矛盾心肠，
任凭那思绪无常之遐想。

但那情书是永恒的见证，
是厚重且不朽之记录者；
是坦诚真相的切实凭证，
是恋人获得安心的庇所；
是其反复斟酌后的执念；
话语飘天际，情书永流传。

163

A Dedication to My Wife
Thomas Stearns Eliot (UK)

To whom I owe the leaping delight
That quickens my senses in our waking time
And the rhythm that governs the repose of our sleeping
time,
the breathing in unison.
Of lovers whose bodies smell of each other
Who think the same thoughts without need of speech,
And babble the same speech without need of meaning...
No peevish winter wind shall chill
No sullen tropic sun shall wither
The roses in the rose-garden which is ours and ours
only
But this dedication is for others to read:
These are private words addressed to you in public.

163

献辞给爱妻
托马斯·斯特恩斯·艾略特（英）

是谁送我的跳跃的喜悦
在醒着时令我感官活跃
我们熟睡时唯从那节拍，
那同呼吸共命运的和谐。
情侣身体散发彼此气息，
不需言语而能想法一致，
无需含意呢喃相同话题……
没有乖戾寒风使之冷凄
没有阴郁热带骄阳凋敝
仅属我们的玫瑰园玫瑰。
但这献辞是供旁人读语：
我赋你的私语尽可昭世。

164

Virginia
Thomas Stearns Eliot (UK)

Red river, red river,
Slow flow heat is silence
No will is still as a river
Still. Will heat move
Only through the mocking-bird
Heard once? Still hills
Wait. Gates wait. Purple trees,
White trees, wait, wait,
Delay, decay. Living, living,
Never moving. Ever moving
Iron thoughts came with me
And go with me:
Red river, river, river.

164

弗吉尼亚
托马斯·斯特恩斯·艾略特（英）

红河啊，红河，
你缓缓而行 激情即是静默
没有什么意志像河一样
安静。热能的涌动
仅仅通过反舌鸟的鸣啭
耳闻过？寂静的山丘
在等待。关口在等。紫树林、
白树林，在等待、等待，
延迟和衰退。活着，活着，
永葆不动。曾经流动的
似铁般意念随我而来
又随我而去：
红河啊，红河～河。

165

The Last Conqueror
James Shirley (UK)

Victorious men of earth, no more
Proclaim how wide your empires are;
Though you bind-in every shore,
And your triumphs reach as far
As night or day,
Yet you, proud monarchs, must obey
And mingle with forgotten ashes, when
Death calls ye to the crowd of common men.

Devouring Famine, Plague, and War,
Each able to undo mankind,
Death's servile emissaries are;
Nor to these alone confined,
He hath at will
More quaint and subtle ways to kill;
A smile or kiss, as he will use the art,
Shall have the cunning skill to break a heart.

165

终极征服者
詹姆斯·雪莉（英）

尘世的胜利者们，别再说
你们帝国的疆域何其辽阔，
虽然你们吞并了每一片海岸，
你们的胜利抵达遥远，
远得堪比昼夜绵延，
但你们 骄傲的君主们，必须服从
当死神呼唤你们身入众生时，
和那被遗忘的遗骸相一气。

那吃人的饥荒，瘟疫和战火，
每一个都使人类毁灭，
那死神的奴性使者，
远不限于这些，
他随心所欲
有着更古怪和微妙的杀人技巧；
一个微笑或亲吻，若施狡技，
狡猾的伎俩会使人心碎。

166

Encounter
Czeslaw Milosz (Poland)

We were riding through frozen fields in a wagon at
dawn.
A red wing rose in the darkness.

And suddenly a hare ran across the road.
One of us pointed to it with his hand.

That was long ago.Today neither of them is alive,
Not the hare, nor the man who made the gesture.

O my love, where are they, where are they going
The flash of a hand, streak of movement, rustle of
pebbles.
I ask not out of sorrow, but in wonder.

166

邂逅
切斯瓦夫·米沃什（波兰）

凌晨我们乘马车碾过霜地。
黑暗中有个红翅腾空升起。

蓦然间，一只野兔蹿过小路，
我们当中有人手指向野兔。

彼时遥远。现他们都已辞世，
野兔消逝，做手势的也已长辞。

我的爱啊，他们在哪？去了何方
挥手瞬间，动作划痕，卵石簌簌声。
我打听是出于惊奇，而非悲怆。

167

In Black Despair
Czeslaw Milosz (Poland)

In grayish doubt and black despair,
I drafted hymns to the earth and the air,
pretending to joy, although I lacked it.
The age had made lament redundant.

So here's the question -- who can answer it --
Was he a brave man or a hypocrite?

167

在黑色绝望中
切斯瓦夫·米沃什（波兰）

在灰色疑惑和黑色绝望中，
我提笔圣歌向土地和天空，
我佯装快乐，尽管快乐拮据。
这时代令抱怨变得多余。

所以这是个问题——谁能答复——
他是勇士还是伪善之徒？

168

Follower
Seamus Heaney (Ireland)

My father worked with a horse-plough,
His shoulders globed like a full sail strung
Between the shafts and the furrow.
The horses strained at his clicking tongue.

An expert. He would set the wing
And fit the bright steel-pointed sock.
The sod rolled over without breaking.
At the headrig, with a single pluck

Of reins, the sweating team turned round
And back into the land. His eye
Narrowed and angled at the ground,
Mapping the furrow exactly.

I stumbled in his hobnailed wake,
Fell sometimes on the polished sod;
Sometimes he rode me on his back
Dipping and rising to his plod.

168

追随者
谢默斯·希尼（爱尔兰）

我爹用马匹拉着犁耕地，
　肩膀鼓圆像个张满的帆
　在车辕和犁沟之间鼓起。
　马儿使劲拉，他呃呃吆唤。

　是行家。他把挡泥板定位
　又安装好那锃亮的钢锋。
　草皮翻过后都没有破碎，
　到地头，他猛拉一把缰绳，

　淌着汗水的马转过马身
　回到田地中。他一只眼眸
　眯成缝，把地线斜着瞄准，
　准确无误地掐算好犁沟。

　我在他钉靴后跌跌撞撞，
　时而跌倒在光滑草皮处；
　时而他让我骑在脊背上
　随着他沉重的脚步起伏。

I wanted to grow up and plough,
To close one eye, stiffen my arm.
All I ever did was follow
In his broad shadow round the farm.

I was a nuisance, tripping, falling,
Yapping always. But today
It is my father who keeps stumbling
Behind me, and will not go away.

我多想会耕地，自己长大，
闭着一只眼，绷紧着胳膊。
　我所能做的只是跟着他
农场里的他那影子绰绰。

我是个讨厌鬼，总是绊倒，
　叽叽喳喳地叫。可是现在
　却是父亲在我身后跌倒
跟随着我，他不乐意离开。

169

The Problem
Thomas Hardy (UK)

Shall we conceal the Case, or tell it -
We who believe the evidence?
Here and there the watch-towers knell it
With a sullen significance,
Heard of the few who hearken intently and carry
an eagerly upstrained sense.

Hearts that are happiest hold not by it;
Better we let, then, the old view reign;
Since there is peace in it, why decry it?
Since there is comfort, why disdain?
Note not the pigment the while that the painting
determines humanity's joy and pain!

169

问题
托马斯·哈代（英）

应该隐瞒此事还是声明——
我们这些信仰证据的人？
四处的瞭望塔敲响丧钟
弥漫着一种阴沉的意蕴，
听说只少数人专心聆听
眼巴巴把他们心弦绷紧。

最快乐的心不靠它支撑；
我们最好让旧观点统治；
既然蕴含和平，为何批评？
既然蕴含慰籍，为何蔑视？
注意，是画本身，而非颜料
决定了人类的悲喜交织！

170

The Self-Unseeing
Thomas Hardy (UK)

Here is the ancient floor,
Footworn and hollowed and thin,
Here was the former door
Where the dead feet walked in.

She sat here in her chair,
Smiling into the fire;
He who played stood there,
Bowing it higher and higher.

Childlike, I danced in a dream;
Blessings emblazoned that day;
Everything glowed with a gleam;
Yet we were looking away!

170

不见自己
托马斯·哈代（英）

这里是陈旧的地面，
被足踏磨损，凹陷单薄，
这里是昔日那门扇
逝者的脚步曾穿过。

她坐在她那椅子上，
对着炉火微微含笑；
弹琴人伫立那地方，
弓拉的曲调高亢扶摇。

我在梦中无邪地起舞；
那天是上帝的恩赐；
一切都有迷光飘浮；
但我们却没有在意！

171

Tears
Walt Whitman (US)

TEARS! tears! tears!
In the night, in solitude, tears;
On the white shore dripping, dripping, suck'd in by the
sand;
Tears—not a star shining—all dark and desolate;
Moist tears from the eyes of a muffled head:
—O who is that ghost? —that form in the dark, with
tears?
What shapeless lump is that, bent, crouch'd there on the
sand?
Streaming tears—sobbing tears—throes, choked with
wild cries;
O storm, embodied, rising, careering, with swift steps
along the beach;
O wild and dismal night storm, with wind!
O belching and desperate!
O shade, so sedate and decorous by day, with calm
countenance and regulated pace;
But away, at night, as you fly, none looking—
O then the unloosen'd ocean,
Of tears! tears! tears!

171

眼泪
沃尔特·惠特曼（美）

眼泪！眼泪！眼泪！
黑夜里孤独流下的眼泪，
纷纷滴落苍岸被沙吮进，
眼泪——星光不见——荒凉漆黑。
湿润的泪从蒙头的眼溢出，
啊，那儿有个幽灵是谁？
那个在黑暗中落泪的身影？
弯腰蹲在沙滩、蓬乱的一堆？
泪崩——呜咽——扎心——噤啕哽住，
啊，风暴兴起激冲海滩上，
啊，疯狂的夜雨风声鹤唳！
啊，呃逆喷涌并令人绝望！
啊，白天影静端庄步伐稳，
而夜晚你飞起不见万类——
啊，那时那是奔放的大海，
眼泪！眼泪！眼泪！

172

A Noiseless Patient Spider
Walt Whitman (US)

A noiseless patient spider,
I mark'd where on a promontory it stood isolated,
Mark'd how to explore the vacant vast surrounding,
It launched forth filament, filament, filament, out of
itself,
Ever unreeling them, ever tirelessly speeding them.

And you O my soul where you stand,
Surrounded, detached, in measureless oceans of space,
Ceaselessly musing, venturing, throwing, seeking the
spheres to connect them,
Till the bridge you will need be form'd, till the ductile
anchor hold,
Till the gossamer thread you fling catch somewhere, O
my soul.

172

一只无言而忍耐的蜘蛛
沃尔特·惠特曼（美）

一只无言而忍耐的蜘蛛，
我见它孤寂地处于岬地，
探索着四周的茫茫虚无，
体内向前发出一根根丝，
绵绵放开，始终不倦加速。

而你，我的魂啊，哪里立身，
你独囚于浩渺的沧海中，
冥思冒险投掷，寻系球形，
直至所需桥梁形成，柔韧锚抓定，
游丝勾住某处，我的灵魂！

173

Life in a Love
Robert Browning (UK)

Escape me?
Never-
Beloved!
While l am l, and you are you,
So long as the world contains us both,
Me the loving and you the loth,
While the one eludes, must the other pursue.
My life is a fault at last, I fear:
It seems too much like a fate, indeed!
Though I do my best l shall scarce succeed
But what if l fail of my purpose here?

It is but to keep the nerves at strain,
To dry one's eyes and laugh at a fall,
And baffled, get up to begin again,-
So the chase takes up one's life, that's all.
While, look but once from your farthest bound
At me so deep in the dust and dark,

173

钟爱一生
罗伯特·勃朗宁（英）

舍我而去？
千万不要——
我的挚爱！
只要我还是我，你还是你，
只要这世界还容纳我们俩，
我钟情而你并不情愿
当一方逃避，另一方必定追逐。
我的一生恐怕终是错误：
这似乎太像命运，确实如此！
虽然我竭尽全力也成功无望。
但倘若我的目的落空又如何？

不过是紧绷神经，
擦干泪水，笑对跌倒，
受挫后，起身再重新开始，
所以这场追逐占尽一生，仅此而已。
然而，哪怕你从最远的地界
向深陷红尘与黑暗的我看上一眼，

No sooner the old hope drops to ground
Than a new one, straight to the selfsame mark,
I shape me-
Ever
Removed!

旧的希望很快破灭
新的希望，径直还朝着同一目标，
我塑形自己——
永远
那么遥远！

旧的希望很快破灭
新的希望，径直还朝着同一目标，
我塑形自己——

174

Prospice
Robert Browning (UK)

Fear death?---to feel the fog in my throat,
The mist in my face,
When the snows begin, and the blasts denote
I am nearing the place,
The power of the night, the press of the storm,
The post of the foe;
Where he stands, the Arch Fear in a visible form;
Yet the strong man must go:
For the journey is done and the summit attained,
And the barriers fall,
Though a battle's to fight ere the guerdon be gained,
The reward of it all.
I was ever a fighter, so---one fight more,
The best and the last!
I would hate that Death bandaged my eyes, and forbore,
And bade me creep past.
No! let me taste the whole of it, fare like my peers,
The heroes of old,
Bear the brunt, in a minute pay glad life's arrears

174

展望
罗伯特·勃朗宁（英）

怕死？——感觉雾气噎喉，
迷雾蒙住我面孔，
当雪花飘落，疾风预示
我在接近那地方，
夜色威力，风暴压迫，
敌人的哨所；
他站立之地，显示极度恐惧；
但是壮士必须前行：
经过旅途到达山巅，
障碍已倒，
但是犒赏前仍有一仗要打，
这仗是一切的报偿。
身为斗士，所以——再打一仗，
正是我绝佳的最后一搏！
我恼恨死神蒙我双眼，容忍
让我悄悄过去。
不！这是让我经历所有，像同龄人们，
古老的英雄一样，
承受打击，瞬间偿付美好生活的亏欠

The black minute's at end,
And the elements' rage, the fiend voices that rave,
Of pain, darkness and cold.
For sudden the worst turns the best to the brave.
Shall dwindle, shall blend,
Shall change, shall become first a peace out of pain.
Then a light, then thy breast,
O thou soul of my soul! I shall clasp thee again,
And with God be the rest!

痛苦，黑暗和寒冷。
突然这最糟之境给勇士赏以最好。
黑暗即逝！
群伙的狂怒，恶魔咆哮，
在减弱，缓和，
变化，最先化为来自痛苦的一种宁静。
然后一束光，还有你的胸膛，
哦，你是我灵魂的归属啊！我要重新抱紧你，
余生和神在一起！

175

If Thou Must Love Me
Elizabeth Barrett Browning (UK)

If thou must love me, let it be for naught
Except for love's sake only. Do not say
'I love for her smile...her look...her way
Of speaking gently,...for a trick of thought
That falls in well with mine, and certes brought
A sense of pleasant ease on such a day'--
For these things in themselves, Beloved, may
Be changed, or change for thee,--and love, so wrought,
May be unwrought so. Neither love me for
Thine own dear pity's wiping my cheeks dry,--
A creature might forget to weep, who bore
Thy comfort long, and lose thy love thereby!
But love me for love's sake, that evermore
Thou mayst love on,through love's eternity.

175

假如你一定爱我
伊丽莎白·巴雷特·勃朗宁（英）

假如你一定爱我，莫需回报
就为爱而爱吧，莫言
"我爱她微笑…她的容貌…她温婉
的谈吐…和心思的巧妙
我们契合无间，当然带来
这般日子里的宜人的轻松"——
亲爱的，这些事物本身，可能
会变，或因你而变—如此铸就的爱，
或许亡尽。也不爱我
只因你用怜悯擦干我的脸颊——
我也许忘却哭泣，因为蒙受
你长久抚慰，因而失去你的爱！
但为爱而爱吧，那会永久
使爱传下去，穿越爱海。

176

Traveling through Fog
Robert Hayden (US)

Looking back, we cannot see,
except for its blurring lights
like underwater stars and moons,
our starting-place.

Behind us, beyond us now
is phantom territory, a world
abstract as memories of earth
the traveling dead take home.

Between obscuring cloud
and cloud, the cloudy dark
ensphering us seems all we can
be certain of. Is Plato's cave.

176

穿过迷雾
罗伯特·海登（美）

回眸望去，我们看不见，
　除了那些模糊的光线
恰似水中朦胧的星月，
　不见我们的起点。

在身后，此刻，视野之外
　是幻影之地，一个世界
抽象得如逝者归乡时
　所携带的尘世的记忆。

在那遮天蔽日的云河
　环绕我们的雾霭的黑色
似乎是我们确信的全部。
　宛如是柏拉图洞穴。

177

A Rondel of Merciless Beauty
Geoffrey Chaucer (UK)

Your two great eyes will slay me suddenly
Their beauty shakes me who was once serene
Straight through my heart the wound is quick and keen

Only your word will heal the injury
To my hurt heart, while yet the wound is clean
Your two great eyes will slay me suddenly
Their beauty shakes me who was once serene

Upon my word, I tell you faithfully
Through life and after death you are my queen
For with my death the whole truth shall be seen
Your two great eyes will slay me suddenly
Their beauty shakes me who was once serene
Straight through my heart the wound is quick and keen

177

无情美人回旋曲
杰弗里·乔叟（英）

你迷人的眸蓦然诛灭我
他们秋波流盼乱我心旌
直击内心伤口迅疾灼痛

只有你的话治愈这伤害
我痛苦的心，趁伤口干净
你迷人的眸蓦然诛灭我
他们秋波流盼乱我心旌

我郑重发誓，赤心相告你
无论生死你都是我女王
我的死亡昭示整个真相
你迷人的眸蓦然诛灭我
他们秋波流盼乱我心旌
直击内心伤口迅疾灼痛

178

The Birds Rondel
Geoffrey Chaucer (UK)

Now welcome Summer with thy sunne soft,
That hast this winter's weathers overshake,
And driven away the longe nighties black.

Saint Valentine, that art full high aloft,
Thus singen smalle fowles for thy sake:
Now welcome Summer with thy sunne soft,
That hast this winter's weathers overshake.

Well have they cause for to gladden oft,
Since each of them recovered hath his mate.
Full blissful may they singe when they wake:
Now welcome Summer with thy sunne soft,
That has this winter's weathers overshake,
And driven away
the longe nighties black.

178

鸟儿回旋曲
杰弗里·乔叟（英）

迎接夏日，你柔和的阳光，
　把冬天冰冷的气候摇落，
　驱赶走漆黑的长夜苍苍。

圣瓦伦丁啊，你高高在上，
　因此小鸟会为你而歌唱：
　迎接夏日，你柔和的阳光，
　把冬天冰冷的气候摇落。

啊，他们常常有理由欢畅，
　为每一个鸟伴侣的重获。
　醒来时它们喜悦地歌唱：
　迎接夏日，你柔和的阳光，
　把冬天冰冷的气候摇落，
　驱赶走漆黑的长夜苍苍。

179

An Octave
Prague in the Golden Autumn
JOHN ZHAO Yizhong (Czech)

The sky is high with pale clouds and cool air;
The Vltava shines the silver light fair.
Waving up and down in the autumn wind,
The white swans swim to and fro pair by pair.
The Skyscraper Tower shows its grand style;
The most beautiful is the Old Town Square.
In the epidemic are few tourists;
The Twin-tower Fane tolls for good luck there.

179

七律
金秋布拉格
（中华新韵）
赵宜忠 JOHN（捷克）

天高云淡气寒清，
塔瓦银光闪闪明。
明暗金风推浪涌，
雌雄白鸟绕河行。
摩云神塔雄姿秀，
夺目骄城广场拥。
瘟疫悲年寥看客，
鸣钟双塔祝昌平。

180

Tonight
JOHN ZHAO Yizhong (Czech)

I feel completely free tonight,
Wielding my sword neath the moon bright.
With none in mind I'm in delight.
Then I invite my friend to wine;
Cup by cup we drink till mid-night.
Chanting poems we are happy quite.

180

浣溪沙
今宵夜
（词林正韵）
赵宜忠 JOHN（捷克）

自在今宵无虑牵，
剑挥月下意悠闲。
心无尘念甚欣然。

而后邀朋来对酒，
几多换盏夜央看。
吟诗佐饮不停欢。